The Pictorial Guide to Garden Flowers

Marshall Cavendish

Published by
Marshall Cavendish Books Limited
58 Old Compton Street
London W1V 5PA

© Marshall Cavendish Limited 1985

ISBN 0 85685 103 5
Printed and bound in Italy by L.E.G.O.

Introduction

This most attractive book has over seven hundred full-colour photographs with accompanying captions. It has been specially designed to enable the reader to identify most of the more common garden flowers and many of the less usual ones too.

The secret lies in the way the book has been compiled. Firstly it is divided into five plant sections ; herbaceous plants, alpines, flowering trees and woody climbers, aquatics and shrubs. Then each plant section is divided into six colours which are themselves divided into sub-sections of size. On the How to use this book page this system is described and explained in detail.

Not only is this a superb reference book it is also a splendid picture book packed with photographs well worth admiring for their own sake. Lovers of flowers and beauty alike will be delighted with this book.

Pictures supplied by:

Alpine Garden Society 42, 93, 102, 131, 132, 141, 220
Amateur Gardening 7, 35, 38, 57, 60, 71, 78, 108, 120, 149, 161, 166, 208
H.R. Allen 203
D.C. Arminson 14, 15, 52, 69, 79, 83, 85, 100, 107, 120, 124, 130, 133, 134, 137, 139, 143, 147, 148, 151, 153, 162, 178, 194, 195, 203, 204, 214, 215, 233
K. Aupiner 226
P. Ayers 36, 101, 122, 125, 153, 186, 228
Barnaby's Picture Library 26
K.A. Beckett 46, 133, 151, 198, 225, 244
R.G. Benfield 87
Carlo Bevilacque 34, 58, 79, 82, 119
T. Birks 94, 120, 226, 233, 236
Blackmore & Langdon 111
D.V. Blogg 96, 99
P. Booth 113, 191, 193
F.W. Buglass 92
J.K. Burras 54, 200, 211
R.J. Corbin 14, 21, 24, 36, 39, 44, 45, 65, 76, 94, 97, 121, 154, 164, 179, 193, 199, 204, 207, 228, 242
J.K. Cowley 53, 168, 209
C.J. Dawkins 155
A.F. Derrick 74
G. Douglas 76, 129
J.E. Downward 16, 47, 53, 60, 70, 100, 102, 112, 121, 149, 156, 157, 190, 209, 223
D. Ewes 15
Valerie Finnis 8, 11, 12, 14, 17, 18, 19, 27, 33, 42, 43, 58, 64, 67, 68, 69, 72, 73, 77, 78, 79, 83, 84, 86, 88, 89, 92, 98, 103, 104, 105, 106, 108, 114, 115, 118, 125, 126, 128, 130, 131, 132, 133, 135, 136, 139, 142, 144, 145, 146, 147, 150, 151,
152, 154, 156, 162, 163, 165, 168, 172, 174, 182, 187, 193, 195, 198, 200, 204, 208, 210, 212, 213, 235
P. Genereux 73, 75, 190, 207, 221, 225, 232, 235, 239
A. Greenway 57
John Groot 54
A.P. Hamilton 66, 95, 140, 210
Iris Hardwick 70, 75, 115, 118, 126, 186, 235
H.R. Hood 20, 217
Peter Hunt 7, 9, 22, 35, 40, 41, 50, 57, 60, 62, 67, 70, 72, 97, 98, 107, 114, 123, 141, 148, 150, 152, 163, 171, 188, 191, 195, 200, 202, 211, 245
A.J. Huxley 16, 32, 44, 45, 76, 80, 85, 88, 96, 100, 101, 110, 119, 122, 141, 144, 169, 177, 181, 184, 185, 188, 202, 205, 212, 213, 229, 236
G.E. Hyde 12, 33, 42, 56, 63, 75, 99, 103, 109, 123, 124, 125, 140, 157, 164, 167, 168, 169, 170, 184, 188, 197, 218, 220, 227, 228, 230, 242
L. Jackson 84
Leslie Johns 18, 31, 53, 87, 126, 134, 210
R. Kaye 23, 78, 132, 134, 137, 138, 140, 153, 155, 222
D.J. Kesby 143, 170, 236
J. Knowles 206
John Markham 9, 13, 14, 32, 74, 112, 128, 176, 180, 181, 186, 191, 192, 231
Elsa Megson 39, 47, 120, 169, 198, 202, 219, 232, 240
National Botanic Gardens 192
Frank Naylor 25, 165, 169, 231
Morris Nimmo 62
S.J. Orme 17, 89, 171, 178, 218, 243
R. Parrett 31
Picturepoint 115
M. Pratt 245
R. Proctor 51, 81, 139, 140, 162, 183
A. de Rahm 115
A. Rainbow 142
C. Reynolds 91, 101
Rodway 172
Rossenwold 99
E.R. Rotherham 105, 234
Iantha Ruthven 179, 224
E.S. Satchill 197, 224, 230
D.J. Simpson 238
Miki Slingsby 109
Harry Smith 8, 9, 10, 11, 12, 13, 15, 18, 19, 20, 21, 22, 23, 24, 25, 26, 28, 29, 30, 31, 32, 34, 36, 37, 38, 39, 40, 41, 43, 45, 46, 47, 48, 49, 50, 51, 52, 54, 55, 56, 57, 58, 59, 61, 62, 63, 64, 65, 67, 68, 69, 71, 74, 77, 79, 80, 81, 82, 83, 84, 86, 87, 88, 90, 91, 94, 95, 99, 101, 103, 104, 105, 106, 110, 116, 117, 118, 119, 121, 125, 127, 128, 129, 131, 135, 136, 137, 138, 140, 142, 143, 144, 145, 148, 149, 150, 154, 155, 156, 157, 158, 159, 160, 162, 163, 165, 167, 168, 170, 172, 173, 174, 176, 177, 179, 1980, 182, 185, 189, 190, 191, 194, 195, 196, 197, 199, 201, 202, 203, 205, 206, 208, 209, 211, 213, 214, 215, 216, 217, 218, 219, 220, 222, 223, 224, 225, 226, 227, 228, 229, 230, 231, 232, 233, 234, 236, 237, 238, 239, 240, 241, 242, 243, 244, 245
Tourist Photo Library 10, 32, 69, 82, 227
A. Turner 134, 135
Colin Watmough 50
L.S. Whicher 142, 146, 237
D. Wildridge 104, 130
C. Williams 55
Denis Woodland 16, 23, 30, 37, 41, 89, 107, 204, 214
K. Woodward 113
W.J. Unwin 34

Glossary

axil   The upper angle between a leaf or leaf-stalk and the stem. Buds growing in the angle are known as axillary buds.

beak   Shaped like a narrow cone or bird's beak.

boss   Central cluster of stamens in a flower.

bract   A scaly or petal-like leaf, often to be found at the base of a flower stalk, or just behind the flower head.

calyx   The outer protective part of a flower, usually consisting of green petal-like organs which may be joined to form a tube.

corymb   A flat or convex cluster of flowers, the stalks of which arise closely one above the other from the top of an erect stem.

cultivar   A coined word to mean cultivated variety. A variety of plant of garden or cultivated origin.

flower-head   A group of flowers together. There are several terms to express the arrangement of flowers in a head, each of which denotes the form and shape, e.g. umbel, spike, panicle.

glabrous   Smooth or without hairs.

hybrid   A cross bred plant. The progeny of two different plants.

keel   The lower two petals of flowers belonging to the pea family. These are pressed together and form a shape resembling the keel of a boat.

lax   Of loose or open growth.

panicle   For the purposes of this book, a comprehensive term which describes any loosely branched spray arrangement of flowers on a plant.

petal   Usually the coloured attractive part of the flower. Where there is one ring of petals the flower is said to be single, where there is more than one ring, double or semi-double.

pistil   The female organ of a flower, consisting of an ovary (which later becomes seed pod), stigma and style.

rosette   A formation (usually) of leaves radiating from a central point to form a circle. Leaf rosettes are nearly always at or near ground level.

solitary   Referring to plants which bear one flower to each stem.

spadix   A fleshy flower-spike typical of members of the arum family. Small flowers are embedded in the lower part, and the tip is often club-shaped. The whole spike is clothed in a spathe.

spathe   A modified leaf or bract which is petal-like and encloses the spadix.

stamens   The pollen-bearing organs which arise from the centre of a flower. The thread-like part is the filament, the head, usually yellow, sometimes coloured, is the anther.

stigma   The tip of the pistil which is usually hairy or sticky to trap the male pollen grains.

style   The stalk which joins the stigma to the ovary.

umbel   A cluster in which the small flower stalks arise from one point at the top of a stem and form a flattish flower-head.

Contents

How to use this book

This pictorial guide has been specially designed to help you identify many of the flowers growing in your garden. In order to do this the book has been divided into five broad categories which need no gardening expertise to distinguish: herbaceous plants, alpines, aquatics, flowering trees and woody climbers, and shrubs. Each of these categories is then further divided into six colour groups and within these colours there are smaller sections based on flower size and plant size. The six colour groups are pink, red, orange and yellow, white green and cream, blue, and purple. The flower and plant sizes — which correspond to mature plants grown on average to good soil under temperate climatic conditions — are as follows:

flower size:	small	Less than 3cm
	medium	3 to 8cm
	large	over 8cm
plant size for herbaceous plants, alpines and aquatics:	small	under 30cm
	medium	30cm to 1.5m
	tall	over 1.5m
plant size for shrubs:	small	under 75cm
	medium	75cm to 2m
	tall	over 2m
plant size for flowering trees and woody climbers:	small	under 3m
	medium	3 to 7m
	tall	over 7m

When identifying a flower the first step is to decide to which of the five main plant categories it belongs. There are certain basic rules to follow which can automatically allocate a plant to its section. For example if the plant is growing on or on the edge of water, or on very boggy ground, it is likely to be an aquatic. In the same way, if the plant is less than 8cm in height it is quite likely to be an alpine. If the plant is neither very small nor beside water, the next thing to decide is whether it is woody. That is to say whether the plant has a sturdy or divided stem. If this is the case then the plant will be either a shrub, a flowering tree or a woody climber. Probably the simplest way to decide between a shrub and a flowering tree or woody climber is on the basis of size: shrubs are likely to be squatter and bushier, and, of course, flowering trees usually have trunks rather than sturdy stems. If the plant is not woody, beside water or very small, it will probably fall into the herbaceous plant category.

Once the plant category has been decided, turn to the right colour section. Remember, however, that many flowers grow in a wide range of colours and in this book it will have been illustrated only in its most common colour or, occasionally, colours. Now establish in which flower size and plant size section the plant falls, and go through until you find the photograph to match your flower. If you do not find it immediately try the appropriate size section of the other colours and, failing that, try the appropriate sections of the other four plant categories in case you have wrongly allocated it in the first place.

HERBACEOUS PLANTS

including bulbs, corms and tubers

PINK
Small Flowers:
Small Plants

Herbaceous plants are those in which the top growth is not woody and dies down at the end of the season. For the purpose of this book the growth is more than 8cm in height, and can vary in texture and spread. The leaves may be quite simple or curiously shaped and can be single or composed of several leaflets arranged together to form a compound leaf.

▲ *Begonia semperflorens* Leaves rounded or heart shaped. Pale flowers with two small and two large petals. Pink in bud, white suffused pink when open. Fluffy yellow anthers in middle. Buds like flat purses in small clusters.

◄ *Bellis perennis* 'Monstrosa Plena' (Double Daisy) Leaves spoon shaped in rosette at ground level. Flowers double daisy-like usually pink or white petals. Solitary, held above leaves.

◄ *Iberis umbellata* (Candytuft) Leaves plentiful, narrow and pointed. Flowers in flattish small heads carried above leaves. Pink, mauve, white. Two small and two large petals. (Also a shrub by species and known as *Iberis sempervirens*).

▼ *Origanum dictamnus* (Dittany of Crete) Leaves conspicuously felted with silver hairs; small, in twos and enfolding the stem. Flowers two-lipped, lower lip larger, stamens protrude from mouth. Flowers in clusters among pink overlapping bracts forming pendulous heads.

▼ *Cyclamen neapolitanum* (Cyclamen) Leaves pointed, heart-shaped or kidney-shaped, very variable, dark green marbled silver. Flowers solitary, folded back. Mouth almost hexagonal, facing downwards. Shades of pink and white.

▼ *Linaria maroccana* (Toad-flax) Leaves narrow, opposite at base of stem, but alternate above. Flowers tubular spurred, two or three colours together, pink, purple, yellow and white. Flowers two-lipped. Lips meet to form mouth.

▲ *Lamium maculatum* (Pink Dead Nettle) Leaves the main feature, heart-shaped, green with central white flash. Flowers surround stems from upper leaf bases, each held in tiny five-pointed cup. Flowers helmet-shaped with darker lower lip.

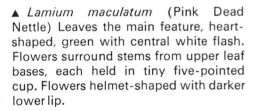

▲ *Geranium psilostemon* (Armenian Cranesbill) Leaves hand-shaped, deeply divided into pointed segments. Flowers magenta, black centres. Veins show on all five petals. Stems thickened at the joints.

▼ *Majorana hortensis* (Pot Marjoram)
Aromatic. Leaves rounded. Flowers in
branched clusters; divided into two lips,
the lower is three-lobed. Found wild on
chalky soils. (Sometimes known as
Origanum onites).

▲ *Malcomia maritima* (Virginian Stock)
Leaves narrow. Flowers in many shades
of pink, mauve and white. Four separate
petals often white at base with yellow
eye. Used as edging in summer.

PINK
Small Flowers: Medium Plants

▶ *Bergenia cordifolia* (Elephant Ear, Megasea or Pig Squeak) Leaves oval to rounded, large, shining, evergreen and leathery. They squeak when rubbed between thumb and finger. Flowers in rounded heads, tubular with five petals, darker centre.

▶ *Clarkia elegans* (Clarkia) Leaves soft green. Flowers in shades of pink and white closely borne along leafy stem. Four petals, somewhat crinkled and pompon-like.

▼ *Chelone obliqua* (Turtle Head or Shell Flower) Leaves in pairs behind flower head, narrow, pointed and with a saw-like edge. Flowers rose to red clustered at top of stem. Upper lip hollow and arched with small open mouth at one end.

▲ *Endymion hispanicus* (Spanish Bluebell or Garden Bluebell) Leaves strapshaped, bright green. Can be mistaken for Bluebell leaves. Flowers pale pink, white or blue. Almost scentless.

▼ *Centranthus ruber* (Red Valerian, Spur Valerian or Pretty Betty) Leaves smooth, pale green, pointed or cleft and in pairs on lower stem. Flowers in rounded terminal clusters; red, pink or white.

▲ *Dicentra spectabilis* (Bleeding Heart) Leaves cut into several lobed grey-green smooth leaflets. Stem erect, arched at the top. Flowers deep pink and white, heart-shaped, hanging in a row from the arched stem tip.

▼ *Dianthus barbatus* (Sweet William) Leaves narrow, pointed and in pairs. Flower stems erect, stiff, with prominent joints. Flowers velvety, in two-colour shades of pink or crimson and white. Flowers in clusters forming a flat head.

◄ *Erigeron* 'Foerster's Liebling' Leaves smooth, small and triangular. Flowers daisy-like, numerous with flattened yellow centre and many petals. Pinks, mauves and purples.

▼ *Filipendula palmata* (Dropwort or Pink Meadowsweet) Leaves maple-like with five pointed lobes, toothed, deeply veined, hairy, white beneath. Flowers fluffy plumes carried above foliage, pink fading to white. Sometimes erroneously called Spiraea.

▲ *Eupatorium cannabinum* (Hemp Agrimony or Thorough Wort) Leaves green, deeply cut, arranged opposite or in rings on stem; slightly downy on under side. Flowers clustered in flattened heads, seed-like in bud. Stems firm and erect.

▲ *Heuchera* hybrids (Heuchera, Alum Root or Coral Bells) Leaves evergreen, rounded, shining with five lobes. Flowers scattered on red/brown erect stems, bell-like, with five petals united at base. Varying shades of pink and red.

▲ *Hyacinthus orientalis* (Hyacinth) Leaves strap-shaped/folded, enfolding a single fat stem. Flowers horizontal bells, recurved petals, heads roll-like, solid. Varying colours, blue, purple, deep red, yellow and white.

▶ *Lathyrus latifolous* (Everlasting Pea) Two, long, pointed leaflets. Plant lax and straggling. Flowers dominated by fan-shaped petals with small overlapping petals in front. Three to six flowers per stem. Stem winged.

▶ *Liatris spicata* (Snakeroot, Blazing Star or Gay Feathers) Leaves flat and narrow. Flowers pink, mauve, or white with fluffy heads on poker-like spikes. Top flowers open first. Petals numerous, long and narrow.

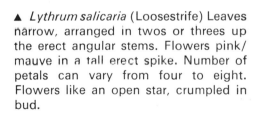

▲ *Limonium suworowii* (Statice or Sea Lavender) Leaves flat, in basal rosette. Stems firm. Flowers very numerous, papery, forming rope-like spikes.

▲ *Lythrum salicaria* (Loosestrife) Leaves narrow, arranged in twos or threes up the erect angular stems. Flowers pink/mauve in a tall erect spike. Number of petals can vary from four to eight. Flowers like an open star, crumpled in bud.

▶ *Physostegia virginiana* (Obedient Plant) Leaves narrow, oblong, toothed and in pairs. Flowers tubular, dilated, rose-pink, hinged on stem. They can be turned to face any direction and will stay there. There is a white form.

▲ *Schizanthus Pinnatus* hybrids (Butterfly Flower or Poor Man's Orchid) Leaves deeply divided, fern-like. Flowers pink or white with yellow/brown markings. Very showy, like faces with open mouths.

▲ *Stachys lanata* (Lamb's Ear or Woolly Betony) Leaves felt-like, grey/white, ground covering. Flower stems erect bearing clusters of small tubular pink-purple flowers.

▶ *Polygonum bistorta* 'Superba' (Bistort or Knotweed) Leaves broad oval, pointed, with marked central vein. Flowers pink in fat spikes at end of stems.

16

PINK
Small Flowers: Tall Plants

▶ *Macleaya cordata* (Syn. *Boeconia cordata*) (Plume Poppy) Leaves large, rounded, deeply lobed, white underneath. Flowers buff pink plumes, like drops of dew in bud, fluffy when open because petals fall off. Sap orange when stem is cut.

▼ *Rogersia pinnata* (Bronze Leaf) Leaves stiff deeply divided into five long leaflets often tinged bronze or crimson, stems bronze. Flowers at head of stem in large clusters. Proud appearance.

PINK
Medium Flowers:
Small Plants

▶ *Dianthus X allwoodii* (Pink: Show Beauty) Leaves blue/grey/green, long and narrow in spikey tufts. Flower-stems swollen at joints, often lax. Flowers fragrant, in a wide range of pinks and white. Variety of markings in darker shades. Petals fringed.

▼ *Godetia cultivars* (Godetia) Leaves plentiful, firm, long and pointed. Flowers showy, funnel-shaped. Colours; red, pink, mauve and white. Four separate petals often with a border in another colour.

▲ *Petunia hybrida* cultivar. Leaves oval to rounded, pale to mid-green, sticky when clasped. Stems spreading in loose tufts, bearing trumpet-shaped flowers all summer. Many colour shades, purple, red, pink, yellow and white; some striped.

PINK
Medium Flowers: Medium Plants

► *Cineraria hybrida grandiflora* (Cineraria) Leaves rough, broadly triangular and floppy. Flowers numerous, daisy-like in large, loose, rounded heads. Colour range; pinks, mauves and white, some two-coloured. Black centres.

▼ *Cleome spinosa* (Spider Flower or Spider Plant) Leaves composed of several long pointed leaflets radiating from top of stalk; pungent smell when bruised. Plants covered with small short spines. Flowers pink or white, many in an elongated cluster. Long spidery stamens.

▼ *Aster novi-belgii* (Michaelmas Daisy) Leaves dark green, smooth, narrow and pointed. Flowers daisy-like with fluffy yellow centres. Many together on branches from upper stem. Red, pinks and mauves. Sometimes with double flowers. Here *Aster* 'Sunset'.

▲ *Cyclamen persicum* (Cyclamen)
Leaves heart-shaped often zoned with
silver or pale green. Flowers shades of
pinks, purples, reds and white, sometimes two-coloured. Flowers solitary,
nodding with petals folded back like a
shuttlecock.

▶ *Cosmos bipinnatus* (Cosmos) Leaves
in thread-like segments, ferny. Flowers
borne singly on end of slender stems.
Colour range; white, pinks, reds,
mauves, of single daisy form, (rarely
double) with not less than eight
separate broad petals (florets). Yellow
central boss. Plant branched.

◄ *Dahlia* 'Warton Jane' (Ball Dahlia) Leaves divided into several oval leaflets, somewhat fleshy. Flowers carried singly on hollow, stout, erect stems. Petals quilled, formally arranged to form a ball. Wide colour range.

▼ *Digitalis purpurea* (Foxglove) Leaves large, crinkled, tongue-like in rosette near ground. Flowers purple to white, thimble-like, pendent, mouths open with strong speckling within. Carried in spires, often more flowers to one side. Lower flowers open first.

▼ *Incarvillea delavayi* (Incarvillea) Leaves shining green, many in pairs forming compound leaf at base of plant. Stems thick. Flowers showy, tubular with five rounded petal-like lobes. Several flowers from top of erect stem.

▲ *Dimorphotheca barbariae* (Cape Mari-gold, Star of the Veldt or Namaqualand Daisy) Leaves lance-shaped, aromatic. Flowers borne singly on long stems, daisy-like with yellow centres. Petals very smooth.

▲ *Phlox paniculata* (Border Phlox)
Leaves simple, opposite on flower stem.
Flowers carried in loose rounded head
on firm stems, each a narrow tube
opening into a very flat five-petalled
flower. Colour range; white, mauve
through pink to coral.

▲ *Pyrethrum roseum* 'Eileen May
Robinson' and 'Kelway's Glorious'
Leaves dark green, fern-like. Flowers
borne singly on tough stems, daisy-like
with pronounced yellow centre. Numerous cultivars. Here, 'Eileen May Robinson' pale pink; 'Kelway's Glorious' dark
rich pink.

◀ *Sidalcea malvaeflora* (Prairie Mallow)
Leaves narrow, clearly defined central
vein; basal leaves resemble those of
buttercup. Flowers in terminal spikes on
wirey stems. Petals sometimes fringed
and crinkled. Several cultivars known.

23

◄ *Lavatera trimestris* (Pink Mallow)
Leaves angular, somewhat like those of
ivy. Flowers showy with wide open
trumpets. Five separate petals attached
at base to central boss. Flowers carried
on upper part of stem between leaves.
There is a white-flowered form.

▼ *Tulipa* 'Dyanito' (Lily Flowered Tulip)
Leaves broad, lance-shaped, pointed
and grey/green. Stem round firm. Flowers solitary flask-shaped in bud; star-
shaped when wide open. Petals red,
glossy, pointed, slightly reflexed. Other
lily flowered tulips can be white, red,
pink, yellow. A bulb.

▼ *Tulipa* 'Peach Blossom' (Double
Tulip) Leaves broad, lance-shaped,
pointed and grey/green. Stems round,
firm. Flowers solitary, cup-shaped and
filled with rows of pink petals. Other
double tulips can be red, yellow, white or
orange. A bulb.

◄ *Veltheimia capensis* (Veltheimia) Leaves oblong with slight wavy edge, glossy above, blue/grey beneath. Stems round, bluish grey and stout. Flowers pendulous when open, held in short broad spike, pink tinged with green. A bulb.

► *Watsonia* hybrids (Watsonia) Leaves sword-shaped, soft. Flowers funnel-shaped, six petals with cluster of anthers protruding. Twelve to twenty-four held on a stem, alternately arranged and forming spikes. Shades of pinks, apricot and copper. A bulb.

PINK
Medium Flowers:
Tall Plants

▼ *Lathyrus odoratus* (Sweet Pea) Leaves grey/green, formed of two oval leaflets and terminating in clinging tendrils. Flowers very showy, fragrant, three to ten per stem in loose spike. Stems tough, slightly ribbed. Large fan-like standard petal behind smaller wings.

▲ *Chrysanthemum* 'Keystone' (Chrysanthemum) An intermediate decorative cultivar with oval, rounded-lobed leaves. Stems erect and woody bearing pompom-like flower heads. Petals firm-textured, numerous, curved inwards, maroon above, silvery beneath.

PINK
Large Flowers: Medium Plants

▶ *Amaryllis belladonna* (Amaryllis or Bella donna Lily) Leaves green strap-shaped appearing after flowers. Flowers trumpet-shaped, with six pale pink fused petals. Three to six flowers bursting from the top of the firm stem. A bulb.

▲ *Crinum X powellii* (Crinum) Leaves numerous, strap-shaped and bright green. Flowers like trumpet lilies varying in colour from white to deep rose pink. Eight to ten open in succession bursting from top of thick stem. The cluster backed by two 'leaves'. A bulb.

▶ *Gerbera jamesonii* (Barberton Daisy or Transvaal Daisy) Leaves hairy in low rosette, very long, sometimes wavy. Flowers solitary, daisy-like, petals narrow. Colour range; pink, apricot, buff and white.

▼ *Paeonia* 'Lady Alexander' (Paeony)
Leaves dark green, firm, finger-like and
plentiful. Flowers on firm reddish stems.
Petals cup-shaped, numerous, inner
ones fringed. Central yellow boss. Buds
form hard pink balls like knobs.

PINK
Large Flowers: Tall Plants

▶ *Lilium pardalinum* (The Panther Lily or Leopard Lily) Leaves in rings around the stem. Flower carried singly on widely spaced stalks at top of stem. Five to eight per stem. Stalks arch. Long-flower buds pendulous. Once open six spotted petals curl back. Anthers orange/brown and protruding. A bulb.

▼ *Nerine bowdenii* (Nerine) Leaves strap-like appear after flowers. Flowers in shades of pink. 'Petals' strap-shaped, curl back like wood shavings; up to eight atop each stem. A bulb.

HERBACEOUS PLANTS
including bulbs, corms and tubers

RED
Small Flowers:
Small Plants

▶ *Pelargonium* 'Red Black Vesuvius' (Dwarf Bedding Geranium) Leaves thick, round, scalloped, with a wide zone suffused with bronze. Flowers firey-red several together in cluster at top of purple/bronze stem. Five rounded petals.

▼ *Sedum cauticolum* Leaves fleshy, cold to touch, blue/green, round/kidney shaped, small and in pairs. Flowers in dense rounded clusters like tiny rose red stars with crimson button-like centres. Stamens protrude giving frothy appearance.

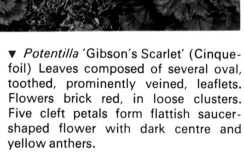

▼ *Potentilla* 'Gibson's Scarlet' (Cinquefoil) Leaves composed of several oval, toothed, prominently veined, leaflets. Flowers brick red, in loose clusters. Five cleft petals form flattish saucer-shaped flower with dark centre and yellow anthers.

RED
Small Flowers:
Medium Plants

▲ *Amaranthus caudatus* (Love Lies Bleeding) Leaves pale green, oval and pointed. Tiny crimson flowers borne in tightly twisted ropes branched, hanging like tails. Flowers can be pale green.

▼ *Astilbe X arendsii* 'Fanal' Leaves decorative, fern-like, divided into several oval, pointed, toothed leaflets. Flowers in feathery triangular plumes composed of myriads of tiny flowers held well above foliage.

▲ *Lupinus* 'Serenade' Leaves divided into several narrow, pointed leaflets arranged like umbrella spokes at the top of the stalk. Flowers in upstanding tapering spikes, each like a boat-shaped pouch with a folded standard petal above, sometimes in two contrasting colours. Wide colour range.

▲ *Lychnis chalcedonica* (Maltese Cross) Leaves oval, rough, in opposite pairs up the erect stems. Flowers bright red, like a five-armed 'cross', together in compact rounded head.

▲ *Polygonum amplexicaule* (Polygonum) Leaves oval, long, pointed and in basal tufts. Flowers tiny, tightly packed in slender spikes on jointed stems, carried well above foliage.

▲ *Stenanthium occidentale* Leaves strap-shaped, slender-pointed, emerging direct from the ground. Flowers sparsely arranged in spikes each flower on a separate angular stem. Pendulous bells with recurved edges. Brownish-purple petals beige at tips redish within. A bulb.

▲ *Pelargonium* 'Black Prince' Leaves fan-shaped, bright green with an irregularly toothed edge. Flowers bronze/red with dark velvety sheen, found together in rounded head. Petals with pale edge, firm and overlapping.

▶ *Pelargonium* 'Decorator' (Geranium) Leaves thick round scalloped edge, central zone suffused bronze. Aromatic. Flowers bright red in clusters forming a head on rigid stalk. Five to ten rounded petals. Several closely allied cultivars have flowers in a range of reds, pinks and white.

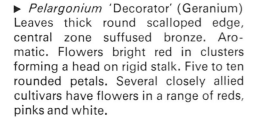

RED
Medium Flowers:
Small Plants

▲ *Viola X wittrockiana* (Pansy) Leaves oval with rounded teeth. Flowers flat borne in the same place as the stalk, five-petalled, rounded velvety, upper ones larger, blotched or striped. Wide colour range.

◄ *Anemone X fulgens* (Scarlet Wind-flower) Leaves deeply divided, fern-like on sturdy stems. Flowers single (rarely double) cup-shaped, scarlet with white centre. Boss of black fluffy stamens.

▶ *Petunia X hybrida* 'Satellite' (Petunia) Leaves pale to mid-green, rounded. Bushy plant. Flowers trumpet-shaped, with a flared mouth alternately striped red and white. Bizarre in appearance. Many other kinds of petunia are grown in a wide colour range.

▼ *Tulipa praestans* Leaves lance-shaped, pointed, clasping stem, grey/green. Flowers vermillion red upstanding goblets with three or four on one stem. Six petals, broad pointed, not shining. Black anthers. A bulb.

▶ *Portulacca grandiflora* Leaves narrow, cylindrical, succulent, arranged in tufts along the stems. Plant spreading and ground-hugging. Flowers double or single, cup shaped, darker centre with satiny texture. Wide colour range; pink, red, orange, yellow and white.

▼ *Potentilla X russellina* (Russell's Cinquefoil) Leaves strawberry-like, composed of three oval toothed leaflets, paler beneath. Flowers pillarbox red, saucer shaped. Five petals rounded and deeply cleft. Black raised centre.

RED
Medium Flowers: Medium Plants

▼ *Knifophia uvaria* 'Spring Time' (Red Hot Poker) Leaves narrow, sedge-like, grey/green in close clumps from ground level. Flowers numerous with pendulous narrow bells, formally arranged in poker-like heads. Upper flowers red, lower ones creamy yellow.

▲ *Gazania X hybrida* (Treasure Flower) Leaves narrow and lance-shaped, dark green above, grey beneath. Flowers daisy-like single, shining and prettily marked with darker zone at base of petals. Showy colour range; pink, red, yellow and mahogany.

▼ *Linum rubrum grandiflorum* (Flax) Leaves small, narrow and pointed alternately along stem. Lax growth. Flowers plentiful, shining red. Five petals opening out flat on sunny days, black centres.

▲ *Lobelia cardinalis* (Cardinal Flower) Leaves dark green, shining, oblong, narrow, in clump at base. Flowers showy, held in tall spike. Three lower petals pronounced and held horizontally away from the flower itself.

▼ *Penstemon* 'George Home' (Penstemon) Leaves long, narrow and pointed. Flowers funnel-shaped with five broad flared lobes, wine red, white scallops within. Black anthers. Showy.

▼ *Monarda didyma* 'Cambridge Scarlet' (Bergamot or Bee Balm) Leaves oval to lance-shaped or in opposite pairs on square sectioned, erect stems. Flowers long, slender, tubular and arching, held in whorls radiating from rounded head.

▼ *Tulipa darwinii* 'London' (Darwin Tulip) Leaves broad, lance-shaped, long, pointed and clasping base of rounded flower stem, greyish green. Six petals, guardsman red, deep goblet-shaped. Yellow anthers within. Many other kinds of Darwin tulip in a wide colour range. A bulb.

◄ *Phygelius capensis* (Cape Fuchsia, Cape Figwort) Leaves shining dark green, oval and in groups along stem. Shrubby growth. Flowers borne in terminal candelabra-like clusters, red, tubular, curved and flared into small lobes at mouth. Pendulous.

RED
Medium Flowers:
Tall Plants

► *Tithonia rotundifolia* 'Torch' (Syn. *T. speciosa, T. tagetiflora*) Leaves heart-shaped, pointed, sometimes three-lobed, largest at the base, smaller up the stem. Flowers resemble dahlias. Petals oval, ribbed daisy-like in formation, boss of golden stamens.

RED
Large Flowers: Medium Plants

▶ *Chrysanthemum* 'Florence Shoe-smith' (Chrysanthemum) Leaves thick, oval with rounded lobes, prominently veined. Flowers like large double daisies, petals reflexed on outer layers. Chestnut red, paler beneath.

▼ *Gerbera jamesonii* (Transvaal Daisy, Barberton Daisy) Leaves form tufted rosette, hairy, long, narrow and sometimes wavy. Flowers large, daisy-like with spikey, narrow petals. In wide colour range all with central pom-pom-like disk.

► *Papaver orientale* (Oriental Poppy) Leaves deeply lobed and toothed, rough, dark green. Plant covered with bristly hairs. Flowers cup-shaped, pillarbox red, floppy, silky texture with black basal blotch. Purple/black boss of stamens.

▼ *Papaver orientale* 'Mrs Perry' (Oriental Poppy) Leaves rough, deeply and sharply lobed and toothed, dark green. Plant covered with bristly hairs. Flowers cup-shaped. Salmon pink to red floppy petals, silky texture. Large black central blotch and boss of black stamens.

► *Gladiolus* 'Oscar' (Large-flowered Gladiolus) Leaves sword-like, held at base in fan formation. Flowers curved trumpets. Petals gently recurved and slightly twisted. Signal red with red/brown splashes. Stamens black, feint buff veination on lower petal at throat.

HERBACEOUS PLANTS

ORANGE & YELLOW
Small Flowers:
Small Plants

▲ *Alonsoa meridionalis* (Syn. *A. mutisii*) (Mask Flower) Leaves opposite along square stems. Flowers dull orange/apricot in loose spikes, short tubular, opening to wide cup with five petals, upper ones largest. Stamen prominent in cup.

▲ *Allium moly* (Yellow Onion) Leaves lance-like, blue/green. Flowers golden yellow, in a six-pointed star with raised centre. Flowers spring from head of stalk to form upstanding bunch. Twelve to fourteen flowers together. A bulb.

▶ *Anthemis tinctoria* (Ox-eye Chamomile) Leaves finely cut and aromatic when rubbed. Flowers daisy-like with double row of petals, bright yellow with yellow centre, carried well above foliage. Cultivars vary from lemon to golden orange.

▲ *Alyssum saxatile* (Gold Dust, Golden Tuft) Leaves small, grey/green, paddle-shaped, evergreen. A loose mat-forming plant. Flowers four-petalled, very small, bright yellow, carried in dense clusters well above foliage.

▼ *Primula vulgaris* (Primrose) Leaves tongue-like, wrinkled, mid-green, paler on reverse. Flowers nestle among clumps of leaves on frail stalks. Pale yellow, fluted trumpet flattened into five cleft petals with central eye.

▲ *Corydalis lutea* (Yellow Fumitory) Leaves small and dainty, deeply divided, pale green. Flowers several together in loose sprays, golden yellow, tubular. Four petals, one spurred at the back like a nib.

▲ *Chelidonium majus* (Swallow-wort, Greater Celandine) Leaves prettily divided, blue/green. Stems hairy, emit yellow juice when broken. Flowers yellow (usually a much brighter yellow than shown here), four-petalled, held in branched sprays. Found wild also.

▼ *Arnebia echioides* (Prophet Flower) Leaves rough and narrow. Flowers bright primrose yellow, tubular with brownish purple spot on each petal when first open (disappears later), sometimes giving a smudged appearance.

▶ *Crepis aurea* (Hawk's Beard) Leaves flat, basal, oval, long, sparce when soil is dry or poor. Flowers resemble small orange/yellow dandelions, carried singly. Particularly numerous when leaf growth is sparce.

► *Euryops acraeus evansii* Leaves silvery white in spikey rosettes tufted growth forming what is strictly a tiny shrub. Flowers bright yellow daisies, particularly found in seaside districts. Petals relatively short compared with the disc.

◄ *Erythronium tuolumnense* Leaves yellow-green, unmottled, broad-pointed and stem-hugging. Flowers golden yellow, solitary, downward-facing like reflexed stars. Six-pointed petals fold away from the golden stamens. Flower stems erect.

43

◄ *Gagea bohemica* Leaves small, grass-like, emerging in sparse tufts from ground level. Flowers somewhat starry. Six tongue-shaped yellow petals, borne in branched clusters on slender, white, hairy stalks. A bulb.

▼ *Limnanthese douglasii* Leaves delicate, fern-like, bright green and plentiful. Flowers shining bright yellow. Five separate petals each broadly edged white. Edges waved, stamens yellow. Flowers are very attractive to bees.

▲ *Hieracium villosum* (Hairy Hawk-weed) Leaves oval, spoon-shaped, blue/green and thickly covered by woolly silver hairs. Stems and buds also covered with hairs. Flowers resemble small dandelions. Petals strap-shaped, numerous, bright yellow.

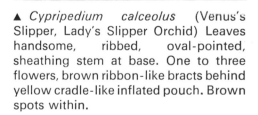

▲ *Cypripedium calceolus* (Venus's Slipper, Lady's Slipper Orchid) Leaves handsome, ribbed, oval-pointed, sheathing stem at base. One to three flowers, brown ribbon-like bracts behind yellow cradle-like inflated pouch. Brown spots within.

▶ *Eranthis X tubergenii* (Winter Aconite) Leaves mid-green, long, narrow, deeply cleft, arranged in a ruff around back of flower. Flowers buttercup yellow. Six rounded petals form cup to hold numerous yellow stamens.

▲ *Narcissus cyclamineus* Leaves small, very narrow, rush-like, bright green emerging from ground. Flowers solitary, lemon yellow, down-facing and tubular in form with wavy edge. Six narrow pointed petals folded back along stem like a crown. A bulb.

◄ *Narthecium ossifragum* (Bog Asphodel) Leaves mid-green, sword-shaped, arranged in basal tuft direct from ground. Usually five straight veins. Flowers yellow, starry with orange anthers, carried on upright spikes. Found in damp situations.

► *Narcissus triandrus albus* (Angel's Tears Daffodil) Leaves sparse, grass-like. One to three flowers together, pendulous, cupped bells, with six-pointed petals reflexed behind and above. A bulb.

▲ *Narcissus bulbocodium* (Hoop Pettocoat Daffodil) Leaves spikey grass-like arising from ground level. Flowers solitary cones of bright yellow backed by spikey petals. Sometimes seen planted in grass. A bulb.

▶ *Nemesia strumosa* (Nemesia) Leaves in twos arranged opposite on stems. Flowers very showy, in range of colours, always with darker centre. Short tubular base with flared mouth. Four-cleft upper lip and bowl-shaped lower lip, sometimes convex.

◀ *Primula X variabilis* 'Pacific Strain' (Polyanthus) Leaves tongue-like, wrinkled, with pronounced vein paler on reverse. Flowers opulent in appearance, velvety. Five petals. Wide colour range with yellow eye. Larger than most Polyanthuses.

47

ORANGE & YELLOW
Small Flowers: Medium Plants

▶ *Isatis tinctoria* (Dyer's Weed or Woad) Leaves mid-green, arrow-shaped and clasping flower stem. Flowers tiny and four-petalled. Anthers give fluffy appearance. Stem simply-branched holds flowers in terminal panicles. Seed pods, black/purple, pendulous.

▶ *Euphorbia robbiae* Leaves in stacked rosettes, oval and dark green. Flowers carried in rounded heads on single stem, three tiny flowers together backed by yellow/green bracts forming a collar.

▼ *Euphorbia epithimoides* (Cushion Spurge) Leaves narrowly oblong, dark green and carried along stem. What appear to be bright yellow flowers are really bracts, tiny flowers nestle at their bases. Flower-heads resemble tiny posies held above hummock of foliage.

▶ *Nonea lutea* (Nonea) Leaves oval, rough, hairy, mid-green. Some dispersed among flowers. Flowers backed by hairy purplish rubbed calyces, rather conspicuous. Flowers yellow, six-petalled, trumpet-shaped. Flower heads nodding.

◀ *Primula* helodoxa (Candelabra Primula) Leaves tongue-shaped crinkled with pronounced central vein. Flowers borne in whorls around erect firm stem at two or three levels forming ruff. Five petals form flat flower with deeper eye.

▶ *Cheiranthus cheiri* (Wallflower) Leaves narrow, pointed, mid-green in bushy tufts. Flowers carried at top of branching stems in small groups. Four petals, velvety, fragrant. Stems strong, colour range; yellow, orange, red.

▼ *Cheiranthus allionii* (Siberian Wallflower) Leaves dark green, narrow, pointed, sparse. Flowers bright orange with four petals, carried in rounded heads on slightly branched stems. Lower flowers fade early and stringy pods appear, upper flowers still in bloom.

▼ *Tanacetum vulgare* (Chrysanthemum Tansy) Leaves fern-like, prettily and deeply divided. Flowers tight golden yellow domed buttons in loose heads at the top of branched stiff stems.

◀ *Lysimachia punctata* (Yellow Loosestrife) Leaves flat, oval, plentiful in fours around lower flower stems. Stems straight and erect. Flowers starry, cup-shaped, bright yellow, with darker centre. Held above foliage in rings on upper part of stem.

▶ *Thermopsis caroliniana* Leaves bright green, oval-pointed, in threes. Flowers borne in erect dense spike, buttercup yellow pea flowers with an erect rounded standard petal and a pouch-like keel.

◄ *Sandersonia aurantiaca* Leaves narrow, sharply-pointed, occasionally ribbed, shining. Flowers with six petals fused to form pendent inflated bell, rounded, bright orange, held singly among leaves at head of stem on wiry stalks.

► *Solidago* 'Crown of Rays' (Golden Rod) Leaves narrow, pointed, plentiful, mid-green. Flowers very numerous tiny yellow daisies forming fluffy sprays. Attract flies. Flower heads resemble feather dusters and are held well above foliage.

ORANGE & YELLOW
Small Flowers: Tall Plants

▶ *Achillea filipendulina* 'Gold Plate' (Golden Yarrow) Leaves mid-green fern-like, plentiful. Stems very tough, rigid. Flowers minute double daisies, hundreds together form plate-like flower-head.

▼ *Ferula communis* (Giant Fennel) Leaves dissected, fern-like, blue/green, jointed. Each joint bound in bract producing side branch. Flowers golden yellow, tiny and numerous in ball-like heads.

▼ *Tropaeolum peregrinum* (Canary Creeper) Leaves blue/green, deeply divided into five lobes. Flowers showy, orange-yellow, bizarre in form. Three fluffy upper petals, two lower ones much larger and deeply fringed, spotted orange at base. Climber.

▲ *Tagetes erecta* 'Cordoba' (African Marigold) Leaves deeply lobed and fern-like, dark green. Stems firm and erect. Flowers deep yellow. Petals numerous, frilled and gathered in tight head. Central eye of stamens. Petals blotched brown.

◄ *Sternbergia lutea* Leaves strap-shaped, narrow, shining and dark green. Flowers six-petalled, funnel-shaped, yellow and resembling the crocus, appear at same time as young leaves. A bulb.

▼ *Tulipa kaufmanniana* 'Johann Strauss' (Waterlily Tulip) Leaves elliptical, broadly folded, like a gutter, striped purple. Flowers solitary on short stalks. Six petals yellow inside, shining blotched mahogany on outside. A bulb.

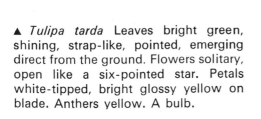

▲ *Tulipa tarda* Leaves bright green, shining, strap-like, pointed, emerging direct from the ground. Flowers solitary, open like a six-pointed star. Petals white-tipped, bright glossy yellow on blade. Anthers yellow. A bulb.

▲ *Rudbeckia* 'Goldsturm' Leaves oval, stiff, pointed. Growth stiff. Flowers borne singly on tough stems, single daisies with spiky narrow petals, butter yellow with ball-like black central boss.

▼ *Sanvitalis procumbens* 'Floro Pleno' Leaves oval, plentiful, soft. Flowers solitary double daisies, centre clustered with brown petals, frilled around by larger-pointed yellow folded petals. Flowers held above foliage in horizontal position.

▲ *Rudbeckia* 'Bambi' Leaves oval, rough and stiff. Growth stiff. Flowers daisy-like, petals elliptical ribbed, acid yellow overlaid mahogany brown at base. Central black boss.

▼ *Petunia* 'Moonglow' Leaves broad/oval, pointed, soft. Stem clammy. Flowers very wide, flared trumpets with recurved mouths, Primrose yellow, scalloped/wavy edges.

ORANGE & YELLOW
Medium Flowers: Small Plants

▶ *Helichrysum bracteatum monstrosum* Leaves narrow, lance-shaped, pointed, pale green. Flowers like large double daisies with almost everlasting petals, borne on erect branched stems. Shades of yellow, red and orange.

▼ *Calceolaria* (Calceolaria) Leaves oval, densely hairy with winged stalks that clasp the stem. Flowers kidney-shaped pouches, usually heavily spotted.

▼ *Verbascum dumulosum* Leaves grey/green, felted, oval, pointed, veined and slightly toothed. Flowers lemon yellow. Five round petals opening flat. Stamens in tiny fluffy protruding bunch.

▼ *Crocus vernus* (Crocus) Leaves grass-like with paler stripe down centre. Flowers in wide variety of colours, often feathered with a second colour. Large golden stigma in the centre.

▲ *Othonnopsis cheirifolia* Leaves flat, paddle-shaped, green/grey, smooth, rather thick, arranged densely on stems. Flowers golden yellow, daisy-like with proportionately large central disc of deeper gold. Spreading habit.

▲ *Eschscholzia californica* (Californian Poppy) Leaves narrowly dissected, fern-like, grey/green. Flowers range through bronze/orange, yellow and ivory. Four petals, shiny and of thin texture. Buds enclosed in green pointed cap or calyx.

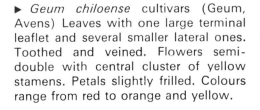

► *Geum chiloense* cultivars (Geum, Avens) Leaves with one large terminal leaflet and several smaller lateral ones. Toothed and veined. Flowers semi-double with central cluster of yellow stamens. Petals slightly frilled. Colours range from red to orange and yellow.

▲ *Inula ensifolia* (Elecampane) Leaves plentiful, narrow, grey/green. Flowers golden yellow daisy-like. Petals in several rows, blunt ended. Central disc prominent, slightly darker golden yellow.

◄ *Asphodeline lutea* (The King's Spear, Asphodel) Leaves narrow and grassy, densely clothing erect stems. Flowers with six distinct spreading petals, bright yellow with central darker line. Stamens prominent, long and curving. In spikes.

▼ *Begonia* 'Lady Roberts' Leaves bright green, shining, roughly heart-shaped but asymetric. Flowers of velvety texture singly or two or three on loosely branched stem. Petals gathered together forming rosette, smooth saucer shape.

▼ *Ursinia anethoides* (Syn. *Sphenogyne anethoides*) Leaves mid-green divided into thread-like segments, feathery. Flowers single daisies, carried singly. Yellows and oranges, always with dark orange zone at the base. Bright orange disc.

▲ *Chrysanthemum segetum* (Annual Chrysanthemum) Leaves deeply divided, almost fern-like. Flowers daisy-like with blunt-ended notched petals; central disc comparatively large, dark, surrounded by concentric zones in a wide range of colours.

▲ *Celosia argentea Pyramidalis* (Syn. *C. plumosa*) (Common Coxcomb) Leaves pale with bright green edges, toothed, heart-shaped. Flowers in full fluffy pyramidal heads resemble feather dusters. Shades of red and yellow.

▶ *Cladanthus arabicus* (Syn. *C. proliferus, Anthemis arabica*) Leaves deeply cleft into narrow segments. Flowers golden yellow single daisies with notched or fringed petals. Held singly at end of simply-branched stems. Strong smelling.

► *Antirrhinum majus* 'Fire King' (Snap-dragon) Leaves dark green, simple, plentiful at base. Flowers tubular, held on firm erect stems in spires, upper and lower petal tips folded back and inflated to form a thick-lipped mouth.

▼ *Coreopsis verticillata* (Coreopsis, Tickseed) Leaves thread-like plentiful dark green. Flowers daisy-like and spikey. Usually seven or nine petals, butter yellow, held on wiry dark stems, centres small, speckled black/brown by dark anthers.

▼ *Doronicum plantagineum* (Leopard's Bane, Danewort) Leaves mid-green, arranged alternately. Lower ones with stalks, upper ones clasping stem. Flowers yellow, single daisies, golden yellow disc.

▲ *Gaillardia* 'Goblin' (Gaillardia) Leaves simple, tongue-like with marked central vein, forming basal clumps. Flowers single daisy-like with distinct numerous petals, deeply cleft. Disc red. Crimson zone at base of each petal.

▲ *Gazania X splendens* (Treasure Flower) Leaves narrow, tongue-shaped above, whiter beneath, simple, darkish green. Flowers single daisies, showy orange, silky, petals with black and white 'jewel' pattern at base. Orange disc. Cultivars in wide colour range.

◄ *Crocosmia masonorum* Leaves sword-shaped, pleated but not too stiff, several arising from same point. Flowers borne in flattened arrow-heads, funnel-shaped tube, six oval unequal petals, spreading.

▲ *Heliopsis scabra* 'Light of Loddon' (Heliopsis, Orange Sunflower) Leaves narrow, rough, bright green, oval and slightly toothed. Flowers golden yellow double daisies with wide frill around, like pompom with ruff. Borne singly at ends of erect stems.

▼ *Helenium autumnale* cultivars (Helenium, Sneezewort) Leaves narrow, mid-green, plentiful and slightly rough. Flowers single daisy-like. Petals notched or fringed and folded back making dark brown disc very prominent. Golden anthers cover disc.

▲ *Gentiana lutea* (Yellow Gentian) Leaves large, ribbed, oval/pointed, stem-hugging with basal rosette. Flowers borne in dramatic spikes, each flower-cluster cupped by small leaf. Flowers five-petalled stars, golden yellow.

▼ *Haplopappus glutinosus* Leaves small, dark green, tufted on shrubby base, slightly toothed. Flowers golden yellow single daisies borne singly on stems. Petals reflexed to make yellow disc protrude.

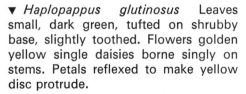

▲ *Heliopsis scabra* 'Golden Plume' (Heliopsis, Orange Sunflower) Leaves narrow, rough, bright green, oval, slightly toothed. Flowers golden yellow, double daisies, petals slightly recurved. Borne at the ends of erect stems.

▲ *Hylomecon japonicum* Leaves slightly toothed, veined, mid-green, five leaflets together form compound leaf. Foliage an attraction of the plant. Flowers yellow, four separate petals with central boss of yellow stamens.

▲ *Meconopsis regia* (Himalayan Yellow Poppy) Leaves stout, lower ones large, narrowly spoon-shaped, covered with bronze/gold hairs. Flowers cupped. Four distinct petals with central boss of golden orange stamens, pronounced pistil.

◄ *Mentzelia lindleyi* (Syn. *Bartonia aurea*) (Blazing Star) Leaves resemble those of thistle. Flowers golden yellow cup-shaped. Five distinct petals each with long point. Cluster of feathery stamens makes centre seem fluffy. Fragrant.

▼ *Oenothera fruticosa* 'Yellow River' (Sundrops, Evening Primrose) Leaves oval to narrow. Flowers plentiful, yellow. Four petals seemingly overlapped until fully open. Eight stamens. Buds often tinged red. Several flowers together in spikes.

▲ *Narcissus pseudonarcissus* cultivar (Daffodil) Leaves strap-shaped, emerging from ground. Flowers golden yellow borne singly with bent necks. Six star-like petals form frill behind trumpet (variable in length) with scalloped edge. A bulb.

▶ *Grindelia chiloensis* (Syn. *G. speciosa*) Leaves elliptical, narrow, nearly clasping stem, glabrous, clammy. Flowers cup-shaped daisies with pointed shiny yellow petals. Centre orange, borne singly on erect rough firm stems.

◄ *Physalis alkekengii* (Chinese Lanterns, Bladder Cherry) Leaves roughly heart-shaped with point, veined, mid-green. Stems twiggy. Flowers white, widely-flared, inflated orange papery lanterns hanging singly. Orange berry inside.

► *Ranunculus asiaticus* (Persian Buttercup, Turban Buttercup) Leaves small, elaborately divided, mid to bright green. Flowers in wide range of colours. Crumpled or folded shining petals. Flowers somewhat frilly with black stamens.

▲ *Sparaxis grandiflora* 'Goldblatt' (African Harlequin Flower) Leaves grass-like flattened, mid-green. Stems wiry. Flowers funnel-shaped, flaring widely into six petals. Buttercup yellow.

▲ *Silphium perfoliatum* (Cup Plant) Leaves the most distinguishing feature — in pairs along the stem forming pointed cup around stem. Flowers daisy-like. Petals long and narrow, ribbed. Central disc acid yellow/green.

▶ *Sparaxis tricolor* (Harlequin Flower) Leaves grass-like flattened. Stems wiry. Flowers funnel-shaped with six flared petals. Three to five flowers together on stem. Central yellow cartwheel mark backed by maroon. Arresting appearance.

▼ *Tropaeolum majus* (Nasturtium) Leaves round, blue/green joined centrally to stem, peppery to taste. Flowers in shades of orange/yellow and apricot, prettily marked, showy. Long spur at back.

▲ *Tritonia crocata* (Syn. *Ixia crocata*) (Blazing Star) Leaves sword-like in fan formation, slightly ribbed. Flowers wide-flaring trumpets. Six broad petals joined at base, each pointed. Yellow anthers.

▼ *Arctotis X hybrida* Leaves oval, basal. Flowers solitary, daisies with silvery shining petals in a wide colour range, yellows, orange, scarlet – all with a darker centre. On a firm stem.

▲ *Trollius europeus* 'The Globe' (Globe Flower) Leaves deeply divided like jagged fingers of a hand. Flowers bright yellow, resemble large semi-double buttercups. Petals numerous overlapped to form compact ball at end of erect stem.

▼ *Venidium fastuosum* (Namaqualand Daisy) Leaves mid-green deeply divided with wavy edges. Flowers daisy-like. Petals narrow, seemingly in two layers. Dark spot at base of each petal. Blue/green central discs. Flowers borne singly.

▲ *Venidio X arctotis* Leaves plentiful at base alternate along stems, much divided mid-green. Flowers solitary spiky daisies in shades of orange, yellow, bronze, mahogany, crimson, pink and ivory white. Usually with contrasting central zone.

▼ *Zinnia haageana* (Zinnia) Leaves oval, dark green, untoothed, pointed, arranged in pairs along stem. Stem rough and erect. Flowers solitary, gaily coloured in combinations of brown, orange and yellow. Petals several, quilled, formal.

▲ *Calendula officinalis* (Marigold) Leaves aromatic, pale green, paddle-shaped. Flowers double daisies in all shades of yellow and orange. Petals very numerous, tightly packed into flower-head. There are single forms.

ORANGE & YELLOW
Medium Flowers: Tall Plants

▶ *Ligularia X hessei* (Giant Ragwort) Leaves large, rough, heart-shaped, stem-hugging. Flowers of irregular daisy form in spikes. Petals yellow, strap-shaped, blunt-ended.

▼ *Ligularia przewalskii* Leaves heart-shaped, edge deeply-toothed, pointed, veins red/purple. Flowers carried in dramatic spire above foliage on brown/purple stem. Flowers yellow, daisy-like, individually untidy.

▲ *Eremurus* Shelford hybrids (Foxtail Lily, Desert Candle) Leaves sword-like, dark green, surround stem base in star-like rosette. Stems erect. Flowers like six-petalled stars. Stamen prominent, arranged in long poker-like spikes.

▼ *Helianthus* 'Loddon Gold' (Chrysanthemum-centred Sunflower) Leaves in threes, oval pointed. Flower-stems erect much-branched. Flowers of many tightly packed petals, ball-like, backed by frill of longer pointed petals.

ORANGE & YELLOW
Large Flowers: Medium Plants

▶ *Centaurea macrocephala* (Yellow Hardhead) Leaves large, long, pointed, with pronounced central vein, closely clothing stem. Flowers like large thistles as big as a man's fist. Brown papery tiled cup carries flowers atop very stout stem.

▼ *Fritillaria imperialis* (Crown Imperial) Leaves slightly fleshy, shining, plentiful along erect robust stem and tufted at top. Flowers hang below tuft in circle of bells. Six-petalled orange or yellow. Clapper of pistil and stamens. A bulb.

▼ *Hemerocallis fulva* (Day Lily) Leaves strap-shaped, pointed and arched. Flowers last one day. Six-petalled, lily-like, trumpet form, petals spreading, somewhat reflexed. Wide colour range, copper, orange, yellow all with central cluster of stamens.

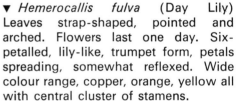

▲ *Lilium pyrenaicum* Leaves shiny, pointed plentiful, lying close to the stem. Flowers held above, two to four per stem, pendulous. Six greenish-yellow petals, speckled brown, folded back and arched to form turk's cap. Bright orange anthers protrude.

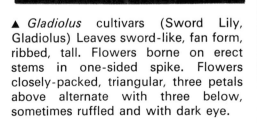

▲ *Gladiolus* cultivars (Sword Lily, Gladiolus) Leaves sword-like, fan form, ribbed, tall. Flowers borne on erect stems in one-sided spike. Flowers closely-packed, triangular, three petals above alternate with three below, sometimes ruffled and with dark eye.

► *Lilium* 'Destiny' Leaves shining, long, pointed, arched clothing length of stem closely. Flowers held upright in twos at top of stem, pure yellow. Six shining petals wide funnel form, chocolate spotting. Stamens with brown anthers.

HERBACEOUS PLANTS

including bulbs, corms and tubers
WHITE, GREEN & CREAM
Small Flowers: Small Plants

▼ *Anemone blanda* (Mountain Anemone) Leaves divided into three deeply cut leaflets, dainty. Flowers more often seen in blue, mauve or pink, like single daisies, bowl-shaped, with about fifteen separate petals. Yellow central eye or disc.

▲ *Anemone narcissiflora* (Narcissus-flowered Anemone) Leaves decorative, deeply divided forming clusters at base. Stems red-tinged, hairy. Flowers in small clusters atop stem. Five white petals sometimes tinged pink. Centre greenish.

▶ *Anaphalis nubigena* (Pearly Everlasting) Leaves grey, felted, narrow, pointed. Flowers papery, white, in starry clusters together at top of stems. Petals small and pointed. Plant erect in habit.

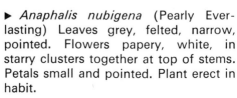

◄ *Anthemis cupaniana* (False Chamomile) Leaves fern-like, lacy, grey, forming cushion below blooms. Flowers single daisies. Petals white and narrow. Disc golden yellow. Flower-stems slender.

▼ *Cerastium tomentosum* (Snow-in-Summer) Leaves covered with silvery white hairs, small, narrow, pointed, forming cushion-like growth. Flowers numerous, covering plant. Five white petals, separate, each cleft.

◄ *Convallaria majalis* (Lily-of-the-valley). Leaves elliptic on short stalks emerging direct from the soil. Flowers pure white rounded bells in a short spike among the leaves. Fragrant.

▼ *Galanthus nivalis* (Snowdrop) Leaves grey-green strap-shaped, blunt-pointed, tending to roll back. Flowers solitary, pendulous like tiny ballerinas bursting from green bead-like cup. Three long oval petals surround three shorter ones marked with green. A bulb.

▼ *Ipheion uniflorum* (Spring Star) Leaves grey/green, grass-like, emerging directly from ground. Flowers solitary, sometimes mauve or bright lilac. Petals joined into a tube at base, flaring into six-lobed star. A bulb.

◄ *Leucanthemum hosmariense* (Alpine Feverfew) Leaves finely cut, silvery green, soft in texture. Flowers dense white daisies with bright yellow discs, held well above foliage and forming a flowery mound.

▲ *Petasites fragrans* (Butterbur) Leaves rounded to triangular, coarse, toothed, reverse thickly felted, boldly veined. Flowers borne on stout stems rising from ground to form club-like heads. Numerous tubular petals bunched together. Fragrant.

◄ *Mitella diphylla* (Mitre-wort, Bishop's Cap) Leaves mid to bright green, round to heart-shaped, three- to five-lobed, toothed. Lobes strongly veined. Flowers held in creamy fluffy heads on slender stems above foliage. Five fringed petals. Stamens spikey.

▲ *Podophyllum peltatum* (Duck's Foot, May Apple) Leaves solitary or in pairs, oval, shining, veined, on erect stem. Flowers solitary, borne between paired leaves, bowl-shaped. Six white petals.

▼ *Reseda lutea* (Wild Mignonette) Leaves divided, narrow and dark green. Flowers fragrant, borne in pointed spikes on firm rough stems. Petals green/yellow and buff. Yellow stamens.

▲ *Spiloxene capensis* Leaves very narrow and grass-like. Flowers solitary like wide-spreading stars. Six long-pointed petals varying from white to pale yellow, boldly blotched at base. Cluster of yellow stamens. A bulb.

WHITE, GREEN & CREAM
Small Flowers: Medium Plants

◄ *Ammobium alatum* (Everlasting Sand Flower) Leaves oblong, basal rosette, stems winged. Flowers silver to white, papery. Prominent yellow disc. Petals numerous, pointed, formally arranged in overlapping rings.

▼ *Alchemilla mollis* (Lady's Mantle) Leaves outstanding attraction, rounded, edges finely toothed somewhat pleated and resembling a cloak. Flowers tiny, cream/green in frothy heads above foliage. Plant downy.

▲ *Anemone X hybrida* 'Honorine Jobert' (Japanese Anemone) Leaves divided into jagged-edged, pointed leaflets. Flowers white (other cultivars are pink). Petals are round and bluntly-pointed. Central disc fringed by conspicuous stamens.

▶ *Artemisia gnaphalodes* (Artemisia) Leaves plentiful, the feature for which the plant is grown. Long and narrow covered with silver-white down. Flowers silver/white, brown-tipped, tiny bobbles in terminal clusters.

▼ *Astrantia major* (Astrantia, Masterwort) Leaves large, deeply divided into five-pointed lobes. Flower-heads carried in twos or threes on branched stems, each one surrounded by papery, silver/ white, star-like ring of bracts. The centre is a cluster of tiny pinkish florets.

▲ *Pelargonium* 'Gonzale' Leaves thick, aromatic, rounded, scalloped, green. Flowers pure white, double rosette of overlapping broad petals. Several flowers together in rounded head.

▼ *Leucojum aestivum* (Summer Snowflake) Leaves strap-shaped, dark to bright green, emerging direct from ground. Flowers white, pendulous, several together at top of stem, bell-like tipped with green, green/yellow within. A bulb.

▲ *Smilacina racemosa* (False Spikenard) Leaves oval, pointed, parallel veins, alternate along firm erect stems. Flowers tiny, borne in dense spiky plumes, creamy/white.

▶ *Chrysanthemum parthenium* (Syn. *Pyrethrum parthenium*)ʼ (Pyrethrum, Feverfew) Leaves bright green, deeply divided, chrysanthemum-like and forming bushy growth. Flowers clusters of small daisies with white petals. Yellow centres raised and conspicuous. Pungent.

◄ *Euphorbia wulfenii* Leaves narrow, bluish-green, long, pointed, with prominent central vein, densely clothing the length of the shrubby stems. Erect sturdy growth. Flowers green/yellow in twos surrounded by bright yellow green bracts which form club-shaped heads.

▼ *Galtonia candicans* (Summer hyacinth, Spire Lily) Leaves long, strap-shaped, emerging direct from ground. Flowers with six fused petals, white, faintly tinged green towards base, often also tipped green, funnel-shaped, pendulous in tall spires. Fragrant.

▼ *Hesperis matronalis* (Dame's Violet, Sweet Rocket) Leaves dark green, shining, long and pointed on erect strong stem. Flowers four-petalled in spikes on branched stems, white often tinged with mauve. Frequently mauve/purple.

◄ *Lysimachia ephemerum* Leaves grey/ green, narrow, pointed, with paler central veins and reverse. Flowers small, five-petalled, white, often tinged purple, carried in long narrow spires on bold erect stems. Plant clump-forming.

► *Molucella laevis* (Bells of Ireland) Leaves bright green, rounded, toothed. Flowers small, white-hooded, tubular enfolded by large, open-mouthed pale green bells, which become paler or buff/cream with age and when dried. Carried in erect spikes.

► *Ornithogalum umbellatum* (Star of Bethlehem) Leaves grassy, shining, bright green, with a silvery central vein, emerging direct from ground. Flowers glistening white wide open stars with six distinct pointed petals. Several flowers together in rounded heads.

▲ *Ocimum basilicum* (Sweet Basil) Leaves main feature of plant, aromatic, highly flavoured, oval, glossy, slightly puckered and sometimes tinged purple on underside. Stem square. Flowers very small, lost among terminal leaves, hooded.

► *Polygonatum multiforum* (Solomon's Seal) Leaves oval, slightly twisted, straight veins, held in pairs in ladder formation along arching stems. Flowers white, green-tipped, in pairs which dangle beneath the arched stem.

82

◄ *Loasa vulcanica* Leaves bright green, divided into three- to five-pointed, broadly toothed, conspicuously veined lobes. Plant armed with stinging hairs. Flowers white, hooded and claw-like arranged in whorls of five at top of stem.

▼ *Veratrum album* (White Hellebore) Leaves handsome, oval, straight-veined and pleated, bright green. Flowers carried well above foliage in dense, branched, rigid plumes. Individual small flowers of six starry petals, cream/buff.

◄ *Tellima grandiflora* Leaves round, scalloped, occasionally slightly pointed, bold radiating veins, sometimes bronze-tinted. Flowers bell-shaped, strung along one side of tall stem, green/white becoming rosy on maturity.

WHITE, GREEN & CREAM
Small Flowers: Tall Plants

▲ *Reynoutria japonica* (Syn. *Polygonum cusidatum*) (Knotweed) Leaves oval, long and pointed, alternating along tough, erect, cane-like stem. Flowers tiny, starry white, borne in clusters together from each of the upper leaf stalk bases.

▼ *Angelica archangelica* (Angelica) Leaves dark green, large, divided into several toothed oval leaflets lower ones often turn yellow as flowering starts. Stems erect, stout-ribbed and yellow-green, in mop heads borne on stalks like umbrella spokes.

▶ *Heracleum montegazzium* (Giant Hogweed) Leaves unequally cut into many toothed segments. Stem very robust, branched in the upper part. Flowers small, white, arranged in large cartwheel-like heads.

WHITE, GREEN & CREAM
Medium Flowers: Small Plants

▲ *Hermodactylus tuberosus* (Syn. *Iris tuberosa*) (Snake's Head Iris) Leaves rush-like, pointed, emerging direct from ground. Flowers with three spoon-shaped petals at points of triangle, purplish black. Claw-like standards bright green. A bulb.

◄ *Zephyranthes candida* (Flower of the West Wind) Leaves grass-like, plentiful, shining and dark green. Flowers with five oval pointed white petals in wide starry cups. Centres depressed, green, encircled by six golden anthers.

▲ *Sanguinaria canadensis* 'Flore Pleno' (Bloodroot) Leaves with grey/blue, kidney-shaped, lobed and toothed, prominently veined. Flowers rosette of tightly-packed pure white oval petals. A single-flowered wild species is also grown.

◄ *Nierembergia repens* (Syn. *N. rivularis*) Leaves thick, bright green, spoon-shaped, several together, emerging from underground stems. Flowers stand away from leaves. White cups with five large spreading lobes. Yellow ring at base.

WHITE, GREEN & CREAM
Medium Flowers: Medium Plants

▶ *Helleborus lividus* Leaves divided into several lance-shaped leaflets like fingers of hand, dark green, plentiful. Flowers in rounded terminal clusters of pale green bells. Yellow/green cluster of stamens within, turning purple-brown with age. Five overlapping petals.

▼ *Campanula latifolia* 'Alba' (Great Bellflower) Leaves oval, pointed, toothed, rough to touch. Flowers in erect terminal spikes, bold white bells with wide starry mouths. Stiff cream 'clapper'-like pistil within.

▼ *Helleborus foetidus* (Bear's Foot, Stinking Helleboro) Leaves like a many-fingered hand, with long narrow toothed leaflets of dark green. Basal leaves evergreen. Flowers palest green, pendulous, rounded bells, several together in terminal heads on erect stems. Stamens white/cream.

▲ *Helleborus niger* (Christmas Rose) Leaves dark green, shining, composed of five oval toothed leaflets on purple mottled stem. Flowers solitary or in twos and threes open bowls filled with cream stamens. Petals egg-shaped, sometimes pointed tinged purple on backs.

▲ *Celmisia spectabilis* (Cotton daisy) Leaves in rosettes, long, narrow, ribbed, glossy, deep green above, covered in silvery or buff below. Stems with small bracts. Flowers solitary, single white daisies with bold yellow disc. Only in mild localities.

▶ *Hyoscyamus niger* (Henbane) Leaves large, jagged in outline with light veins. Stem stout and rigid. Flowers cream/brown with dark veins, saucer-shaped with five rounded deep scallops. Brown throat. Yellow/green/purple stamens.

▼ *Rheum alexandrae* (Alexandrian Rhubarb) Leaves large, shiny, oval, tough with broad cream veins. Flowers cream, borne on tall spike protected conspicuously by cream/lemon hooded bracts.

▲ *Nicotiana alata grandiflora* cultivars (Tobacco Plant) Leaves oval, pointed, roughly-veined, borne horizontally. Flowers with very long tubes, also held horizontally. Five oval pointed petals making flat flared mouth.

▲ *Morina longifolia* (Himalayan Whorlflower) Leaves thistle-like, dark green with narrow spiney saw-like edge. Flowers borne in long spikes held in clumps of green prickly bracts forming rings at intervals around stem. Tubular, white, tinged rose.

WHITE, GREEN & CREAM
Medium Flowers: Tall Plants

▶ *Eremurus elwesii* 'Albus' (Foxtail Lily, Desert Candle) Leaves narrow, tapering to a point, in spreading basal rosette. Flowers fragrant, six-petalled pink or white stars borne in poker-like spikes. Stamens long, slender and protruding.

► *Impatiens roylei* (Syn. *I. Glandulifera*) (Policeman's Helmet or Himalayan Balsam) Leaves oval, bright green, arranged alternately on robust, erect, succulent stems. Flowers red-purple, pink or white, helmet-like. Two recurved petals below flaired rounded petal. Pink speckles on yellow throat.

▲ *Yucca flaccida* (Yucca, Adam's Needle, Bayonet Plant) Leaves sword-like in basal rosette, often grey/green and with thread-like filaments on the margins. Flowers white/cream borne in arresting branching spikes. Pendulous waxy bells with pointed petals.

► *Yucca aloifolia* Leaves sword-like in a dense rosette on a short trunk. Flowers bell-shaped, in a branched spine from the centre of the leaves.

WHITE, GREEN & CREAM
Large Flowers: Medium Plants

▲ *Arisaema candidissimum* Leaves large, arrow-head-shaped and shining. Flowers cornet-shaped. Spathe (like a large petal), ribbed green above and suffused green/brown at base, enfolds a central upstanding club-like organ (spadix). Flowers borne singly.

◄ *Arum creticum* Leaves like large arrow-heads, shining metallic and dark green. Flowers cream to yellow, veined towards base brown/purple. Single 'petal' (spathe) enfolds pencil-like spadix. Spathe pointed and folded back. Stems sturdy. Flowers borne singly.

◄ *Calochortus nitidus* (Mariposa Lily) Leaves strap-shaped. Flowers white with three rounded triangular petals (often yellow). Petals with purple blotch and yellow hairs, three lower ones much smaller (sepals). Six stamens and triangular green centre. A bulb.

▼ *Crinum moorei* (Crinum) Leaves wide strap-shaped, long, arching, pointed. Flowers six to eight in a terminal head on stout thick leafless stem. Six white or pink blunt-ended petals open wide and recurved. Pretty stamens and wire-like upward style. A bulb.

◄ *Crinum asiaticum* (Asiatic Poison Bulb) Leaves wide, strap-shaped, arching. Flowers fragrant, white, up to forty in cluster. Six petals, narrow, spreading, recurved, sometimes flushed pink. A bulb.

▼ *Lilium regale* (Lily) Leaves dark green, narrow, pointed and densely borne on stout erect stem. Flowers white with yellow shading in throat, purple/red outside, trumpet form. Six petals. Golden anthers. Fragrant. A bulb.

▼ *Papaver orientale* 'Perry's White' (Oriental Poppy) Leaves deeply lobed, rough, dark green. Plant covered with prickly hairs. Flowers white, frilly petals silky-textured, cupped. Purple/black basal blotch and boss of stamens.

◄ *Paeonia obovata* 'Alba' (Peony) Leaves firm in texture, deeply divided into leaflets, suffused bronze when young. Flowers bowl-shaped, opening out when weather is warm. Petals pure white, central boss of cottony stamens and purple stigmas.

► *Panacratium maritimum* (Sea Lily) Leaves grey/green strap-shaped. Flowers sweetly-scented, several together atop fat round stem. Chunky upright trumpets with pointed edges, backed by six narrow pointed petals, like daffodils. A bulb.

WHITE, GREEN & CREAM
Large Flowers: Tall Plants

▲ *Cardiocrinum giganteum* Leaves large, shining, green, heart-shaped, on stalks forming basal tuft with smaller ones up stem. Flowers fragrant, white with wine red markings inside. Long six-petalled trumpets, pendulous in terminal spires. A bulb.

◄ *Asphodelus cerasiferus* (Syn. *Aramosus*) Leaves sword-like, central vein keeled. Flowers six-petalled wide stars borne in branched spikes, striking and decorative. Petals white, sometimes brownish at the base.

▲ *Zantedeschia aethiopica* (Arum Lily, Calla Lily) Leaves shaped like spearhead, green. Flowers with large white spathe (petal-like leaf) pointed and recurved enfolding yellow club-like (spadix). For mild localities. A bulb (tuber).

▶ *Romneya coulteri* (California Tree Poppy, Canyon Poppy, Matilija Poppy) Leaves grey to blue/green deeply lobed. Flowers fragrant, solitary. Petals, satiny in texture, rounded and crinkled. Central globular golden boss of stamens.

HERBACEOUS PLANTS

including bulbs, corms and tubers
BLUE
Small Flowers: Small Plants

▲ *Ajuga reptans* 'Variegata' (Bugle). Leaves oval, light green, edged with cream. (Most forms are without the edging.) Creeping habit, flower-stems upstanding. Flowers tubular, with flared lips, forming little mouths, borne in spike.

◄ *Anagallis linifolia* (Blue Pimpernell). Leaves small, oval to lance-shaped, pointed in small tufts. Flowers with five petals, bright rich velvety blue above, red/purple beneath. Centre orange/red 'pepperpot' ribbed. Range of colours: red, rose/purple, blue.

▲ *Chionodoxa luciliae* (Glory of the Snow) Leaves strap-shaped, bright green, emerging directly from ground. Flowers borne in close terminal clusters, open, starry, pale blue or pale mauve, white-centred with six petals. A bulb.

▶ *Myosotis alpestris* (Forget-me-not) Leaves oblong, with central vein, forming tufts. Flowers pale blue, pink in bud. Five joined petals fall as scalloped collars. Tiny yellow eye.

▼ *Lobelia tenuior* (Blue Lobelia) Leaves small, narrow, pointed, toothed or deeply lobed, forming small tufts or trailing clumps. Flowers tubular with prominent flared mouth. Three upper petals arched, three lower ones larger and hanging. Shades of blue.

▲ *Heliophila longifolia* Leaves grasslike, sometimes lobed, bright green. Flowers dainty. Four rounded petals with square yellow eye. Flowers on short stalks, borne in open spikes.

▼ *Muscari neglectum* (Muscari, Grape Hyacinth) Leaves narrow, dark green, like gutter in cross section, emerging directly from ground. Flowers closely clustered cups to form elongated drumstick-like spikes. Dark blue. A bulb.

▶ *Specularia speculum* (Syn. *Campanula speculum*) Leaves oval, pointed, larger at base. Flowers found singly on branched stems forming loose head. Five blue/mauve rounded petals with central marked white eyes and white stamens.

▼ *Phacelia campanularia* Leaves oval, with irregular rounded teeth, aromatic when bruised. Flower-stems simply branched, reddish. Flowers intense blue, widely funnel-shaped with upstanding mouth. Five rounded, flared petals. Five prominent white anthers protruded.

▲ *Nemophila menziesii* (Baby Blue Eyes) Leaves soft-textured, deeply dissected and lobed. Flowers solitary in upper leaf axils. Five rounded petals, light blue with white eye. Distinctive pointed sepals with lobed appendages.

▼ *Scilla sibirica* (Siberian Squill) Leaves strap-shaped, emerging direct from the ground. Flowers with six-pointed wide-open nodding Prussian blue bells, three or four together on a stem. Yellow stamens within.

▲ *Symphyandra wanneri* (Pendulous Bell Flower) Leaves lance-shaped, irregularly toothed, hairy, lowest ones stalked. Flowers blue to purple/blue long hanging bells with scalloped edge. Calyces green/purple and five-pointed, like cap above bell.

▼ *Synthyris platycarpa* Leaves round, toothed, fringed with hairs, somewhat concave, bright green. Flowers borne closely in spikes at top of stem, tubular, violet blue, with protruding stamens. Calyces purple.

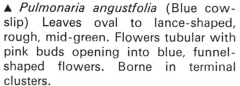

▲ *Pulmonaria angustfolia* (Blue cowslip) Leaves oval to lance-shaped, rough, mid-green. Flowers tubular with pink buds opening into blue, funnel-shaped flowers. Borne in terminal clusters.

▼ *Scilla peruviana* (Cuban Lily) Leaves strap-shaped, tapering, pointed, in a star-shaped rosette direct from the ground. Flowers with six-petalled stars, in tight, broadly-conical head, borne on stout erect stem. A bulb.

BLUE
Small Flowers:
Medium Plants

▲ *Commelina coelestis* (Blue Spiderwort) Leaves lance-shaped, wavy-margined, tapering to point, stem clasping. Flowers carried singly on short upper stems to form loose clusters. Three petals, two upper ones bend backwards, lower one slightly cupped.

◄ *Anchusa azurea* (Syn. *A. italica*) (Italian Bugloss) Leaves rough, hairy, rich green. Flowers vivid blue, carried in loose spikes above foliage, very striking. Cultivars in various shades of blue. Five rounded joined petals form bowl-shaped blooms.

▲ *Echium plantagineum* cultivar (Purple Viper's Bugloss) Leaves oblong, prominently veined, and rough textured. Flowers tubular, expanding at the mouth, borne in branched clusters. Colour range; blue, purple, red, pink and white.

▲ *Echinops ritro* (Globe Thistle, Steel Thistle) Leaves large, prickly, jaggedly lobed. Flower-stem rigid, grey/green. Flowers tiny, tubular. Thread-like twisted petals and protruding styles forming globular head. Metallic blue in bud.

◄ *Echium vulgare* (Viper's Bugloss) Leaves rough, oblong to lance-shaped with prominent mid-rib. Whole plant bristly and hairy. Flowers tubular with lopsided mouth, bearing five lobes. Pink in bud, bright blue when open. Five stamens and style protrude.

Endymion non-scriptus (Syn. *Scilla nutans*) (Blue Bell, Wild Hyacinth) Leaves strap-shaped in basal tufts. Flowers in a somewhat one-sided spike with a nodding tip. Pendulous, narrow, blue-purple bells. Six petals fused and recurved. Pink and white forms are grown. A bulb.

▼ *Eryngium giganteum* Leaves smooth, bright green, heart-shaped. Metallic, highly decorative filaments form starry ruff round thimble-like blue flower-head of many small flowers (not here in bloom). Stamens protrude.

▲ *Gentiana aesclepiadea* (Willow Gentian) Leaves lance-shaped, tapering, symmetrically veined, in pairs horizontal to stem. Flowers dark blue with five-petalled open funnels. Petals pointed, borne on slender arching stems.

▶ *Hybanthus floribundus* (Syn. *Lonidium floribundum*) Leaves bright to mid-green, smooth and narrow. Flowers elaborate, numerous, pale blue, tubular with large shell-like lower lip. Petals marked purple, yellow within.

▼ *Myosotidium hortense* (Syn. *M. nobile*) (Chatham Island Forget-me-not) Leaves oblong, tapering, symmetrically veined to form ridges. Flowers forget-me-not-like but much larger. Five rounded blue petals with white margins.

▼ *Linum narbonense* (Blue Flax) Leaves grey/green, small, very narrow, held erect. Flowers rich bright blue, borne along arched branches. Five rounded petals, slightly arched back.

▲ *Salvia farinacea* (Mealy Cup Salvia, Mealy Sage) Leaves oval, narrow, somewhat aromatic. Flowers in long slender spikes, tubular with a hooded upper and spreading lower lip, deep violet blue. Whole plant is mealy or floury.

▼ *Scabiosa caucasica* (Scabious) Leaves dark green, deeply cleft into narrow segments, basal leaves form a tufted clump. Flower-stems slender, erect. Flowers solitary, numerous. Petals crimped, surrounding a pincushion-like centre.

▲ *Nigella hispanica* (Love-in-a-Mist, Devil in the Bush) Leaves divided into thread-like segments, the upper ones almost obscuring numerous flowers. Petals pointed and arranged like ruff around upstanding stamens and pistil.

▼ *Salvia haematodes* Leaves large, broadly oval, heart shaped at base, hairy and with a corrugated surface. Flowers violet blue, funnel shaped with a hooded upper and spreading lower lip, carried in loose erect spikes.

BLUE
Medium Flowers:
Small Plants

▲ *Aster novi-belgii* 'Audrey' (Michael-mas Daisy) Leaves narrow, dark green, long and pointed, thickly clothing stems and forming dense clump. Flowers daisy-like lavender/mauve with numerous petals and disc yellow. A dwarf cultivar. A wide range of colours is grown.

▲ *Primula bhutanica* Leaves tongue-like with predominant pale veins and toothed edge. Flowers tubular, opening out flat like a primrose, azure blue with orange yellow eye. Five notched petals, velvety in texture.

▶ *Iris histrioides* hybrid 'Lady Strawley' Leaves rush-like. Flowers royal blue. Three lower arm-like petals in triangular formation, each with a rounded tongue-like tip. White flecked centre. Narrower central petals arched upwards. A bulb.

BLUE
Medium Flowers: Medium Plants

▲ *Aconitum carmichaelii* (Monkshood) Leaves deeply indented like fingers of a hand. Flowers violet-blue, borne in spikes. Upper petal forms a helmet, sheltering the rest of the flower.

◀ *Agapanthus campanulatus* (Syn. *A. mooreanus*) (African Lily) Leaves strap-shaped, arching, shining green, in basal tufts. Flowers bluebell blue, many in rounded head on stiff erect stalk.

▼ *Catananche caerulea* (Cupid's Dart)
Leaves hairy, very narrow. Flowers solitary, blue/purple, appearing semi-double. Petals numerous and strap-shaped. Centre purple-black speckled with yellow anthers. Papery silver bracts behind flower-head.

◄ *Cichorium intybus* (Chicory, Succory) Leaves oblong at base, upper ones clasping stem, all rough beneath. Stems also rough. Flowers like bright blue dandelions, rarely white or pink, closed at mid-day. Petals numerous, strap-shaped, notched at tips.

▲ *Delphinium brunonianum* Leaves musk-scented, basal ones kidney-shaped with five-toothed lobes, higher ones three-lobed or entire. Flowers somewhat hooded, resembling monk's hood, spurred, light blue shading to purple. Golden yellow throat. Short branched spikes.

◄ *Erigeron speciosus* hybrid 'Festivity' (Fleabane) Leaves lance-shaped, tapering to the base, borne along erect stems. Flowers like thick tufted daisies, many narrow lilac blue petals. Central disc yellow. Many similar cultivars in shades of blue to pink are grown.

BLUE
Medium Flowers:
Tall Plants

▼ *Delphinium* 'Silver Moon' Leaves dark green, deeply divided, like fingers of a hand. Profuse at base. Flowers frilled clusters of silvery blue petals with a white to cream centre.

▼ *Delphinium* 'Daily Express' Leaves dark green, deeply divided, like fingers of a hand. Profuse at base. Flowers frilled clusters of clear sky blue petals, spurred behind. Centre velvety brown to black.

► *Ipomoea tricolor* (Syn. *rubro-caerulea*) (Morning Glory) Leaves heart-shaped and pointed. Growth slender, climbing. Flowers intense blue, trumpet-like with flared mouths. Some forms have a white or pale blue eye, often with long rays.

▼ *Symphytum X uplandicum* (Hybrid Comfrey) Leaves oval to lance-shaped, larger at base of plant. Flowers in clusters of long bells, wider at the mouth. Pink in bud turning purple or blue/purple on maturity. Whole plant rough and prickly.

BLUE
Large Flowers: Medium Plants

▶ *Meconopsis betonicifolia* (Syn *M. baileyi*) (Blue Himalayan Poppy) Leaves oval to oblong, toothed, basal ones stalked. Flowers deep sky blue with four rounded petals having satin sheen. Yellow boss of stamens. On limey soils the petals will be a paler mauve/blue.

▼ *Iris* 'Patterdale' (Tall Bearded Hybrid Iris) Leaves grey/green, broad, sword-like, forming bold clumps from which the erect stout flower stems arise. Flowers powder blue, flamboyant. Three large pendulous tongue-like lower petals with marked golden beard near base. Three upper petals arch inwards to form a dome.

HERBACEOUS PLANTS

including bulbs, corms and tubers
PURPLE & LILAC
Small Flowers:
Small Plants

▲ *Ageratum houstonianum* (Syn. *A. mexicanum*) (Floss Flower) Leaves heart-shaped, somewhat crinkled, dark green, in basal clusters. Flowers pink to powder blue pompom-like, tiny held in dense heads.

◀ *Fritillaria meleagris* (Snake's Head Fritillary, Chequered Daffodil, Guinea Flower) Leaves grass-like. Flowers purple/brown rounded bells, distinctly chequered, from top of erect stems, pendulous like lamp shades. A bulb.

▲ *Lathyrus vernus* (Spring Pea) Leaves of two soft, pale green, long, narrow leaflets. Flowers purple or pink pea-like in small groups, each with fan-like upstanding standard petal and a bell and wings below.

▼ *Brachycome iberidifolia* 'Purple King' (Swan River Daisy) Leaves divided, thread-like segments, ferny. Flowers stand above foliage, solitary, daisy-like, soft velvety. Petals ribbed and blunt-ended. Disc brown.

▲ *Omphalorgramma vinciflorum* (Syn. *Primula vinciflorum*) Leaves tongue-like spoon-shaped, distinct mid-rib in basal rosette. Flowers nodding, solitary, tubular, with notched tongue-like violet petals (like periwinkle).

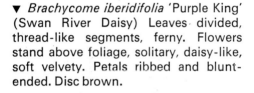

▼ *Salvia horminium* (Clary) Leaves heart-shaped, clothe the upright stem. Flowers small, borne below papery, coloured bracts of purples, mauves and pinks which occur in clusters at the tops of the stems.

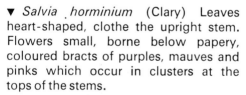

◄ *Viola gracilis* hybrid Leaves oval, with rounded teeth. Flowers solitary, on slender stem. Five triangular petals, four upper ones in square formation, fifth below. Centre eye marked black and yellow.

► *Viola odorata* (Sweet Violet) Leaves heart-shaped, pointed, folded when young. Flowers fragrant, solitary, 'faces' with spur behind. Five petals, upper ones upstanding, two as 'wings' and fifth rounded below.

◄ *Viola tricolor* (Heartsease, Wild Pansy) Leaves oval to lance-shaped, with rounded teeth. Flowers in purple and yellow, sometimes with ivory white. Five petals, marked with black at base resembling 'face', shortly spurred behind.

PURPLE & LILAC
Small Flowers: Medium Plants

▲ *Camassia leichtlinii* (Quamash) Leaves strap-shaped, pointed, emerging from the ground. Flowers in cylindrical spikes, well above foliage. Six pointed petals form star, petals twist together as flower fades. A bulb.

◄ *Eryngium X oliverianum* (Sea Holly) Leaves spiny, thistle-like and somewhat twisted, ruff of narrow silver/mauve filaments surround flower-head. Flowers purple, arranged like pins in a pincushion-like head.

▲ *Geranium pratense* (Meadow Cranes-bill) Leaves hand-shaped, on long stalks divided into seven lobes cut and toothed. Flowers purple/blue saucer-shaped, in loose, terminal clusters. Five petals, rounded, separate. Central pointed style.

▼ *Heliotropium peruvianum* (Syn. *H. arborescens*) (Heliotrope, Cherry Pie) A shrubby plant. Leaves oval, pointed with strong veining. Flowers small, in clustered heads, fragrant, purple to blue/purple, occasionally white.

▲ *Fritillaria pyrenaica* Leaves narrow, strap-shaped, blunt points. Flowers solitary, rarely in pairs. Stem tips curved to hold hanging, large bells. Six broad petals, flared at mouth, somewhat chequered; maroon and olive green.

▼ *Hosta fortunei* (Funkia, Plantain Lily) Leaves oval/heart-shaped, pointed, boldly veined and sometimes with lighter marking. Flowers horizontal to pendulous, slender trumpets, in somewhat one-sided spike, often arched at tip. Lilac.

▲ *Malva sylvestris* (Mallow) Leaves, deeply cleft, general outline triangular, veined. Flowers trumpet-shaped, five cleft petals, lilac/rose with purple veining. Central stalked knob of stamens.

▼ *Lunaria biennis* (Honesty) Leaves dark green, coarse, heart-shaped with jagged edges. Flowers in loose, branched spikes, from main stem, purple/rosy lilac, occasionally white. Four rounded petals. Distinctive silvery oval seed pods.

▲ *Hyssopus officinalis* (Hyssop) Leaves aromatic, small, oblong, in small clusters around woody erect stems. Flowers violet/purple in dense spikes, brownish bracts behind. Tubular, with larger lower lip. Stamens protrude.

▼ *Malope trifida* (Malope) Leaves rounded, soft in texture, sometimes three lobed. Flowers trumpet-shaped, silken, five triangular petals, marked to suggest fluting, rose/purple, pink or white. Three heart-shaped bracts behind.

▲ *Matthiola incana* (Stock) Leaves simple, paddle-shaped, the edges waved, grey, downy. Flowers very fragrant and showy, borne in dense spires. Petals, four if flower single, numerous if double, in posy-like clusters, sometimes with crimped margins.

▼ *Mentha spicate* (Mint) Leaves strongly aromatic, oblong, pointed, toothed and veined. Flowers tiny, lavender/mauve in short spikes, branched at summit of square sectioned stems.

▲ *Mertensia virginica* (Virginian Cowslip) Leaves grey/blue, somewhat fleshy, oval, stalked, smooth. Flowers purple/blue, in graceful drooping clusters, cornet-shaped, mouth often crimped.

▼ *Nepeta X faassenii* (Catmint) Leaves aromatic, small, grey/green, downy, oval, toothed edge. Flowers borne in loose spikes, lavender blue, tubular, two-lipped. Stems square-sectioned.

▲ *Verbascum phoeniceum* 'Lilac Domino' Leaves oval and in basal tufts. Flowers saucer-shaped, with five rounded somewhat wavy-margined, rose-petals. Borne in erect branched spikes.

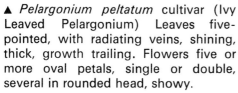

▲ *Pelargonium peltatum* cultivar (Ivy Leaved Pelargonium) Leaves five-pointed, with radiating veins, shining, thick, growth trailing. Flowers five or more oval petals, single or double, several in rounded head, showy.

▲ *Scabiosa atropurpurea* (Sweet Scabious) Leaves lance-shaped, often cut into narrow lobes. Flowers pom-pom-like or pincushion-like, borne on slender erect stems. Found in shades of pink, red, purple and lavender.

▲ *Wulfenia carinthiaca* Leaves form basal rosette, tongue-like, stalked. Flowers violet/blue, borne in soft spikes, individual flowers drooping on maturity, tubular, four spreading lobes at mouth, the upper one toothed.

◄ *Verbena rigida* (Syn. *V. venosa*) (Verbena) Leaves in pairs, long, pointed, elegantly toothed. Flowers claret/purple in rounded heads on tough, branched stems. Small, five round-pointed petals, like star with a deeper centre.

PURPLE & LILAC
Small Flowers: Tall Plants

▲ *Silybum marianum* (Milk Thistle, Holy Thistle, Blessed Thistle) Leaves in basal large rosette, jagged, oval, shining, dark green with broad white veins. Stem spined. Flowers mauve, thistle-like, surrounded by long pointed bracts.

▼ *Veronica exaltata* (Spiked Speedwell, Veronica) Leaves lance-shaped, sharply toothed, smaller and narrower ascending stem. Flowers small, soft blue with prominent stamens carried in long, tapering, erect spikes.

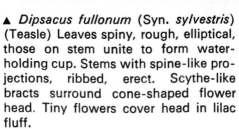

▲ *Dipsacus fullonum* (Syn. *sylvestris*) (Teasle) Leaves spiny, rough, elliptical, those on stem unite to form water-holding cup. Stems with spine-like projections, ribbed, erect. Scythe-like bracts surround cone-shaped flower head. Tiny flowers cover head in lilac fluff.

PURPLE & LILAC
Medium Flowers: Small Plants

▶ *Colchicum autumnale* (Autumn Crocus, Naked Ladies) Leaves absent at time of flowering, lance-shaped, glossy, in clusters of two to four. Flowers goblet-like emerging direct from ground. Six long petals unite to form narrow tube at base. Lilac, yellow anthers. A bulb.

▶ *Crocus tomasinianus* (Crocus) Leaves grass-like, mid-green with silvery central stripe. Flowers and leaves emerge direct from ground in white papery sheath. Flowers goblet-like, six-pointed petals lilac/purple. A bulb (corm).

◀ *Anemone coronaria* De Caen hybrids (Floris Anemone) Leaves deeply cut, ferny, dark green. Flowers solitary, on erect stems above a ring of three stalkless leaves. Single (as here) or double. Centres a boss of velvety black stamens Petals broadly oval, in shades of purple, red, white.

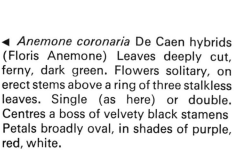

123

▼ *Lathraea clandestina* (Blue Toothwort) Leaves scale-like, yellow/brown, mainly underground. Flower clusters spring straight from soil around roots of willow, poplar and other trees. Flowers tubular, boldly hooded, upright, purple. A parasitic plant.

▲ *Merendera montana* (Syn. *M. bulbocodium*) Leaves follow the flower, very narrow, curved. Flowers erect, funnel-shaped, emerge from ground level, rose/lilac, rarely white.

▼ *Petunia X hybrida* Leaves oval, soft, somewhat sticky, hairy. Flowers showy, slightly floppy, trumpets with flared mouths. Wide colour range in shades of purple, red, lilac, white and pale yellow.

▲ *Viola X wittrockiana* (Pansy) (A hybrid group of plants derived from Viola tricolor) Leaves oval, with broad rounded teeth. Flowers open, flat, in the same plane as the stem. Five-petalled, upper two largest, rounded velvety, black blotch at base of lower three. Often two colours in one flower.

▲ *Platycodon grandiflorum* (Balloon Flower, Chinese Bell Flower) Leaves oval, firm, the lower ones in whorls around stem. Flowers erect violet/blue wide open bells with fountain-like style in centre. Buds inflated like balloons. Pink and white cultivars are grown.

▼ *Romulea clusiana* Leaves resemble fine grass. Flowers six petals, wide, funnel-shaped, on very short stem near ground. Violet/mauve, with white zone in centre and prominent yellow base. A bulb.

▲ *Pulsatilla vulgaris* (Pasque Flower) Leaves dissected, fern-like, woolly. Stem leaves behind flower like silken feathers. Flowers goblet-shaped, in shades of purple to red/purple, silky. Six petals and golden boss of stamens within.

▼ *Primula auricula* (Auricula) Leaves spoon-shaped, smooth, grey green, in rosettes covered (as is the stem) with waxy, white powder, often removed by rain out of doors. Flowers velvety, flat, formal, scalloped in two colours regularly placed.

PURPLE & LILAC
Medium Flowers: Medium Plants

▶ *Aquilegia hybrids* (Columbine, Granny's Bonnets) Leaves dainty, deeply divided. Flowers often of two colours, in a wide range. Five pointed sepal-like petals form background frill to five contrastingly quilled rounded petals, each spurred at back.

◀ *Acanthus spinosus* (Bear's Breeches) Leaves thistle-like, shining dark green, deeply lobed and irregularly cut, each division ends in spine. Flowers white and purple, hooded tubes, borne on striking spikes among elegant green bracts.

▼ *Arctotis X hybrida* Leaves oval/oblong. Grey/green, edge toothed. Flowers solitary, daisy-like, pale violet. Silky petals curve from the central boss of acid yellow. Stamens, small and black. Close in the evening.

◀ *Callistephus chinensis* (China Aster) Leaves oval, coarsely toothed, somewhat ragged edge. Daisy-like flowers, here single, more often double, pompom-form, often seeming ragged and too heavy for flower stems. Wide range of colours.

▶ *Campanula medium* (Canterbury Bell) Basal rosette of leaves, oval to lance-shaped, rounded, toothed, smaller on flowering. Flowers large, shades of pink and mauve, bell shaped, ribbed, flared five lobed mouth. Yellow style split into three at the top.

▲ *Freesia X kewensis* cultivars (Syn. *F. X hybrida*) Leaves sword-shaped, pointed, finely ribbed. Flowers trumpet-shaped with flared mouth of six rounded petals, often two shades, wide colour range. Very fragrant. Flowers borne on one side of stalk, balanced within calyces.

▲ *Campanula glomerata* (Clustered Bellflower) Leaves oval/heart-shaped, toothed edge, become smaller and somewhat clasping on stem. Flowers on erect stems, in tight globular head, bell-shaped with five-pointed petals at mouth. Blue/purple or white.

▶ *Centaurea dealbata sternbergii* (Persian Knapweed) Leaves long, narrow, deeply lobed, irregular edge, green/silver above, white beneath. Flowers thistle-like, tufted. Rose crimson with lighter centre. Petals fringed.

◀ *Helleborus orientalis* (Lenten Rose) Leaves dark green, hand-shaped, composed of several strongly toothed, lance-shaped leaflets. Flowers with five broad cup-shaped petals, variable in colour, green/black to rose/purple, sometimes spotted darker.

▼ *Senecio elegans* Leaves oval, deeply cut into narrow lobes, carried thickly on flower-stem. Flowers single, daisy-like, (sometimes double). Petals, purple to pink in varying shades, centre yellow. Borne in loose clusters on branched stems.

▼ *Penstemon hirsutus* (Syn. *P. pubescens latifolius*) Leaves oblong to lance-shaped. Flowers with gradually inflating tube, widening where the mouth divides into a two-lobed upper lip and three-lobed lower lip. Bearded inside, pale purple to dull violet.

▲ *Tradescantia X andersoniana* (Syn. *virginiana*) (Spiderwort) Leaves strap-shaped, curved, pointed. Flowers in groups, enfolded by two leaf-like bracts resembling clock hands at 6 o'clock. Purple, blue, cerise and white cultivars are available. Three petals set in triangle, centre clustered. Yellow stamens. Buds surround flowers.

▼ *Stachys macrantha* (Syn. *Betonica macrantha* and *B. grandiflora*) (Betony) Leaves elongated, heart-shaped, scalloped edge, rather hairy. Flowers borne in whorls, many together in oblong head, inflated, tubular, broadening to mouth with three-lobed lower lip. Rose and purple flowered sorts are grown. Stem square.

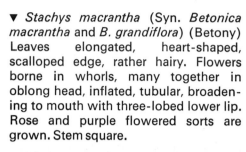

▲ *Xeranthemum annum* (Everlastings) Leaves resemble grey/green grass. Flowers solitary, bowl-shaped daisies, both single and double in wide colour range. Papery texture, which persists after maturity. Central disc appears fringed.

ALPINES
PINK
Small Flowers: Small Plants

Strictly speaking an alpine is a plant whose natural habitat is the high mountainous regions. For the purpose of gardens, however, alpines are plants of low growth persisting from year to year. They may be ground-covering, cushion-like in growth, trailing or like small shrubs.

▲ *Asperula suberosa* (Pink Woodruff) Leaves small, very narrow, white, woolly, arranged in rings around the slender stems. Mat forming. Flowers very small but in abundant clusters, long tubed stars of glowing pink.

▲ *Acantholimon venustum* Leaves needle-like, silver grey, in loose-tufts forming a springy cushion plant. Flowers small rose pink stars. Five petals spread wide, borne in a one-sided spike above foliage.

◄ *Androsace lanuginosa* (Rock Jasmine) Leaves silver, hairy, small, oval to lance-shaped, pointed, òn prostrate stems which form tangled mats. Flowers in rounded heads on erect wiry stalk, flat, resembling buttons with red eye.

▲ *Aethionema* 'Warley Rose' Leaves blue/green, somewhat succulent, narrow. Growth rather shrubby with much-branched stems. Flowers deep pink in clusters atop stalks, freely produced. Four petals; cruciform.

▲ *Dianthus alpinus* Leaves deep green, small, narrow, in opposite pairs forming mats. Flowers comparatively large, flat, circular with serrated edges varying in colour from purple/red, pink to white. Central ring specked with crimson.

▼ *Dianthus* 'La Bourboulle' Leaves grey/green, long, narrow, pointed, forming a neat cushion of growth. Flowers borne singly on short stems, upturned pentagons with fringed edges, deep pink. Protruding stamens.

▲ *Calandrinia umbellata* Leaves dark grey/green, pointed, narrow, succulent and forming rosettes, Flowers bowl-shaped, startling magenta, carried in slightly arching sprays.

▼ *Douglasia nivalis* Leaves narrow, tongue-shaped, slightly downy, clustered to form hummocks. Flowers cupped, nestling above the tufts, stemless, small. Five spreading, oval, pale pink petals with deeper central portion.

▶ *Erinus alpinus* Leaves narrowly spoon-shaped, deeply-toothed forming tufts. Flowers in short spikes on wiry stems borne in profusion, bright pink. Five petals, the three lower spreading. There is a white form.

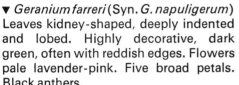

▼ *Geranium farreri* (Syn. *G. napuligerum*) Leaves kidney-shaped, deeply indented and lobed. Highly decorative, dark green, often with reddish edges. Flowers pale lavender-pink. Five broad petals. Black anthers.

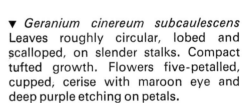

▼ *Geranium cinereum subcaulescens* Leaves roughly circular, lobed and scalloped, on slender stalks. Compact tufted growth. Flowers five-petalled, cupped, cerise with maroon eye and deep purple etching on petals.

◀ *Geranium dalmaticum* Leaves decorative, glossy, roughly rounded, deeply lobed and notched. Sometimes flushed red, hummock-forming. Flowers five-petalled, substantial in texture, bright shell pink.

133

▲ *Gypsophila repens* 'Rosea' Leaves grey/green, narrow, pointed, carried in pairs along wiry stems which branch irregularly and form wide mats. Flowers copiously carried, studding the whole plant with tiny pink five-petalled flowers.

▲ *Lewisia cotyledon hybrid* Leaves tongue-like somewhat fleshy. Flowers carried well above basal rosette, saucer shaped on maturity. Petals strap-shaped, here pink edged white. Colours vary from apricot to rose pink and salmon.

▶ *Petrocallis pyrenaica* Leaves very small, wedge-shaped, three- to five-lobed, in clustered rosettes to form a cushion of moss-like growth. Flowers vanilla scented, cruciform, here pink, often lilac-pink, numerous, carried in small, stalked clusters.

◀ *Oxalis articulata* (Syn. *O. floribunda*) Leaves clover-like on slender stalks, fold together at night. Flowers resemble small funnels with five oblong, spreading petals. Deep rose pink darker eye.

▲ *Primula minima* Leaves glossy, wedge shaped, notched into several points at the flattened tip. Flowers rose pink, flat, petals deeply notched and almost forked. Flowers carried on very short stems, solitary.

▲ *Potentilla nitida* 'Rosea' Leaves clover-like grey/green, silky and hairy. Growth is mat-forming. Flowers rose pink with a darker eye. Five separate, broad, rounded petals, usually notched.

▲ *Phlox adsurgens* Leaves oval, shiny in loose tufts. Trailing stems. Flowers carried in loose terminal clusters. Narrow tube behind wide spreading star. Five oval spreading petals, pale pink with a darker zone on each.

▶ *Primula allionii* Leaves grey/green, broadly spoon-shaped, slightly sticky to touch, forming hummocks. Flowers cover the whole plant. Clear deep pink, but varying, with white base to the five deeply-notched petals.

▲ *Saxifraga grisebachii* Leaves tongue-like, encrusted with lime in neat, compact rosettes. Flowers pink, hidden in red bracts and inflated cups (calyces) carried in nodding heads. Stalks and flower-heads covered in crimson hairs.

▼ *Saxifraga moschata* hybrid 'Edie Campbell' Leaves bright green, cleft into three narrow segments. Growth cushion-forming, springy. Flowers soft pink, wide, cup-shaped. Five rounded petals each marked with crimson blotch.

▲ *Saxifraga X jenkinsae* Leaves small, grey/green, wedge-shaped, in dense cushions, neat. Flowers solitary, on short stems studded all over basal growth, cup-shaped, pale pink with crimson throat.

▼ *Saxifraga oppositifolia* Leaves rigid, wedge-shaped, small, crowded on slender creeping stems. Growth dense, mat-forming. Flowers cup-shaped, petals rounded, shades of pink to red purple, also white.

▶ *Silene schafta* Leaves small, downy, long, oval, pointed, growth tufted. Flowers solitary or two to a stem. Five wedge-shaped petals deeply cleft. Clear pink, darker towards base, set in tubular calyx.

▼ *Sempervivum arachnoideum laggeri* (Cobweb House Leek) Leaves oval in tight spherical rosettes, flattened at the top, and covered with woolly cobweb-like hairs. Flowers five-pointed stars, carmine pink, in small clusters.

▼ *Silene acaulis* (Moss Campion, Cushion Pink) Leaves small, bright green, narrow, pointed, forming generous cushions. Flowers vivid pink, five-petalled with hollow centre and set in reddish, inflated, goblet-like calyx.

▼ *Silene elizabethae* (Syn. *Melandrium elizabethae*) Leaves narrow, lance-shaped, rounded at tips, in opposite pairs. Flowers comparatively large. Five violet/purple petals, fan-shaped. Notched narrow base held in calyx.

137

ALPINES

ORANGE & YELLOW
Small Flowers:
Small Plants

▼ *Hacquetia epipactis* (Syn. *Dondia epipactis*) Basal leaves trifoliate, forming tufted clump. Green/yellow bracts resembling petals form ruff behind the flower head. Flowers yellow, tiny, clustered in posy fashion and fluffy with protruding stamens.

▲ *Draba rigida* Leaves small, narrow, bristly, stiff, arranged in compact cushions. Flowers numerous, in clusters on slender stems above foliage, bright yellow. Petals somewhat squarish. Four in cruciform position, shining, golden yellow.

▼ *Saxifraga X apiculata* Leaves small, bright green, narrow, sharply pointed and forming hummocks. Flower stems with tiny pointed leaves growing flat to stem. Flowers in small clusters, open funnel-shaped, primrose yellow, deeper at the heart.

► *Oxalis chrysantha* Leaves clover-like, forming mats of pale green. Flowers buttercup yellow, solitary, funnel-shaped. Five petals rounded and spreading, soft in texture, with tiny sheaf of golden stamens in centre.

▼ *Potentilla crantzii* (Syn. *Palpestris*) Leaves hand-like, pointed and with five oval-toothed leaflets. Flowers saucer-shaped shining yellow. Five rounded petals, well separated at base, with darker central blotch.

▲ *Morisia monantha* (Syn. *M. hypogaea*) Leaves dark green, narrow, divided into rows of triangular lobes and forming flat dense rosettes. Flowers conspicuous, on very short stalks. Four rounded bright golden yellow petals.

► *Erysimum rupestre* (Alpine Wallflower) Leaves long, narrow, bright green, covering low mound of twiggy growth. Flowers sulphur yellow, in a profusion of clustered heads. Cruciform, petals round and smooth.

▲ *Saxifraga aizoides* (Yellow Mountain Saxifrage) Leaves small, bright green, narrow, fleshy and almost cylindrical. Mat-forming, stems lax. Flowers starry, five well separated pointed shiny petals, often red spotted. Orange and red forms are known.

► *Teucrium polium* Leaves grey/green, slightly woolly, toothed, long, oval, blunt. Rather twiggy bush-like plant. Flowers small, borne in dense rounded clusters, tubular and spiked with protruding styles, giving pincushion effect when in full flower. Also pink and purple.

▼ *Lotus cretica* (Trefoil) Leaves, smooth, grey/green. Composed of three oval leaflets and two leafy stipules where stalk joins stem. Flowers golden yellow in small clusters, resembling miniature sweet peas.

▼ *Parnassia fimbriata* Leaves slightly fleshy, pointed, heart shaped and forming basal rosette. Flowers saucer-shaped with five spreading petals fringed towards the base, golden/apricot dot on each. Spreading stamens in centre.

▲ *Sempervivum grandiflorum* Leaves oblong to oval, with brown-purple, pointed tip, slightly curved and hairy, arranged in symmetrical rosettes. Flowers star-like. Petals narrow, pointed, spreading, pale sulphur yellow, brown at base. Spreading stamens. Plant has resinous smell.

140

WHITE, GREEN & CREAM
Small Flowers: Small Plants

▲ *Aethionema iberidium* Leaves blue/grey narrow, somewhat fleshy. Growth shrubby, neat, with much-branched stems. Flowers numerous, chalk white. Four petals, many in clusters at end of stem.

▲ *Claytonia virginica* (Spring Beauty) Leaves narrow, pointed, mid-green, somewhat fleshy. Flowers starry, fragile. Five petals, pointed. Yellow central boss of stamens. Buds somewhat inflated, held horizontally.

▼ *Anacyclus depressus* Leaves divided into narrow branched segments, fern-like. Growth prostrate, dense, in mats. Flowers daisy-like with yellow central disc. Petals crimson beneath, white above, borne on slender stems which turn upwards.

▼ *Erigeron mucronatus* Leaves small, narrow, pointed. Growth running, foamed with frail blooms. Flowers daisy-like on wiry stems, white, pink, red on the same plant.

▲ *Dianthus* hybrid 'Charles Musgrave' (Musgrave's Garden Pink) Leaves grey/green, narrow, pointed, in tufts forming flattish mats. Flowers appear circular with fringed edges, flat, white with green eye. Many similar cultivars in shades of pink and red.

▲ *Leontopodium alpinum* (Edelweiss) Leaves hoary, grey, narrow, pointed; mostly basal, smaller along stem. Flower-heads like small flannel starfish, felted, grey/white. Yellow clusters of anthers within.

▶ *Hutchinsinia alpina* Leaves small, dissected, in compact rosettes, dark green. A really miniature plant. (Here magnified.) Flowers with four petals, clear white, in clustered heads. Yellow stamen within the cross of the petals.

◀ *Gentiana saxosa* Leaves small, spoon-shaped, shiny, somewhat arching, fleshy, forming low hummocks; flowering stems with smaller narrow leaves. Flowers cup-shaped, white, borne one to five per stem (usually solitary). Six separate spoon-shaped petals with five cream stamens.

◄ *Minuartia laricifolia* Leaves narrow, thread-like, grey/green. Growth lax and prostrate cushion-forming, spangled with numerous blooms. Flowers white, like dainty stars with widespread points. Cluster of yellow stamens in centre.

► *Ourisia macrophylla* Leaves oval, rounded-toothed. Flower stems erect. Flowers in clusters or irregular whorls. Five petals, two upper ones close together and three lower ones spreading. Yellow hairs in the throat.

◄ *Paronychia argentea* Leaves silver grey, small, narrow, mat-forming. Flowers inconspicuous, lacking petals, in small clusters surrounded by comparatively large, white, leaf-like bracts which give the plant a translucent appearance.

143

▲ *Saxifraga granulata* (Meadow Saxifrage) Leaves thick, scalloped, kidney-shaped. Few branched, erect stems bear flowers. Flowers pure white, funnel-shaped with five oval shining petals, yellow at the base.

▲ *Oxalis adenophylla* Leaves grey/green crinkled, like open fans, composed of up to twelve narrow leaflets. Flowers atop stems, one to three together, large, funnel-shaped, cream to pink with a maroon eye.

▼ *Sedum hispanicum* Leaves narrow, small, almost cylindrical, grey/blue sometimes shading to pink at tips. Stems closely packed, prostrate and trailing forming tangled carpet of growth. Flowers spiky small stars.

▼ *Petrocosmea kerrii* Leaves somewhat fleshy, felted, pointed, heart-shaped. Flowers resemble violets. Two upper petals together and three lower ones spreading. Yellow eye.

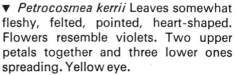

▶ *Sempervivella alba* Leaves broadly oblong and succulent, red-tinged. In tight rosettes, mat-forming. Flowers white, stiff, stars, six to eight pointed. Buds pink-tinged. Base of petals darker. Central yellow boss of pistil and stamen.

► *Tanakaea radicans* Leaves evergreen, somewhat fleshy, oval, with irregularly serrated edges, rounded or heart-shaped at base. Flower stems arch above foliage. Flowers minute, fluffy, cream/white borne in loose spire. Stamens prominent giving foamy appearance to the flower clusters.

WHITE, GREEN & CREAM
Small Flowers: Medium Plants

◄ *Saxifraga longifolia* Leaves greyish, strap-shaped in broad rosette, encrusted silver. Flower-stems arch and branch outwards. Flowers starry, shining, white, copiously borne in thick pyramid, clothing stems to the base.

▲ *Saxifraga cotyledon* Leaves in basal rosettes, tongue-like, finely toothed and rimmed with silver. Flower-stems reddish, arched in great flow of bloom. Flowers fragrant, numerous, starry. Five narrow petals with brownish eye.

WHITE, GREEN & CREAM
Medium Flowers: Small Plants

▲ *Dryas octopetala* (Mountain Avens) Leaves oval, scalloped edge, glossy dark green marked central vein, forming a wide mat. Flowers bowl-shaped, wide. Eight bluntly-pointed petals, clear white, yellow at base, with clustered golden stamens.

▲ *Lewisia columbiana* Leaves in loose rosette, broad, narrowly oval, shining, fleshy. Flowers white or pink — here a white form — in sprays. Wide-spreading, several narrow petals. Central yellow stamens.

ALPINES
BLUE
Small Flowers: Small Plants

▲ *Eritrichium nanum* (King of the Alps) Leaves narrow to oval, pointed, forming dense silvery hairy cushion. Flowers brilliant sky blue. Five rounded petals opening flat, joined, borne in flattish small clusters. Golden yellow eye.

◄ *Cyananthus lobatus* Leaves small, oval. Growth tufted, plants prostrate. Flowers deep violet blue, with five tongue-shaped petals joined together and held behind in a hairy cup (calyx). Flowers numerous. There is a white form.

► *Gentiana septemfida* Leaves lance-shaped pointed, glossy, in basal tufts. Flowers in clusters at top of stem, and in upper leaf axils, trumpet-shaped, blue-purple or deep blue. Five or seven flared petals at mouth. White spots inside.

BLUE
Small Flowers:
Medium Plants

► *Omphalodes cappadocica* Leaves bright green, heart-shaped, pointed, evenly veined. Stalked, rising from ground level. Flowers in graceful sprays, forget-me-not-like in form and colour. Five rounded bright blue petals with lighter eye.

▲ *Omphalodes luciliae* Leaves elliptic, blue/grey, smooth-edged, pointed. Flowers pink in bud, turn soft blue on maturity. Shallow bowl-shaped, breaking into five broadly rounded petals with central rib. Opalescent in appearance.

▼ *Gentian acaulis* (Trumpet Gentian) Leaves oval to lance-shaped, pointed, in opposite pairs, arranged in hummocks or mats. Flowers deep blue trumpets, tube rather straight then flaring into flat five-pointed rim. Frequent green speckles within the throat.

▶ *Gentiana lagodechiana* Leaves oval, pointed, opposite along stems forming upstanding tufts. Flowers deep blue, solitary, upstanding and often freely produced. Short trumpet-shaped, breaking into five widely spreading pointed petals.

▼ *Gentiana sino-ornata* Leaves narrow and pointed borne on trailing stem. Flowers royal blue, very wide upstanding trumpets, opening into five-pointed rim. Lilac/white stripes within throat, and also on outside.

▼ *Gentiana X macaulayi* Leaves narrow and pointed, on prostrate or semi-prostrate stems. Flowers upstanding deep blue trumpets, borne singly flaring into five broad pointed petals. Throat white striped purple within.

▲ *Gentian verna* (Spring Gentian) Leaves rich green, oval to lance-shaped, pointed. Growth loosely tufted. Flowers solitary, numerous, starry when looked upon from above, deep azure blue. Five widely spread rounded petals.

▲ *Houstonia Serpyllifolia* (Syn. *H. caerulea*) (Bluets) Leaves spoon-shaped, small, bright green, forming tufts or low hummocks. Flowers like four pointed stars of china blue. There is a white-flowered form, also one of darker blue.

▼ *Lithospermum diffusum* 'Heavenly Blue' Leaves elliptic to oblong, hairy and rough, numerous, on prostrate mat-forming stems. Flowers in terminal clusters, tubular to trumpet-shape. Spreading at mouth into five rounded petals. Intense blue. Most flowers clustered along stems.

◄ *Jankaea heldreichii* Leaves oval, thick, frosted with silver hairs. Backs of leaves rusted in appearance. Flowers violet/blue, usually two per stem. Rather like a large open-mouthed violet and borne horizontally. Four round petals with darker eye.

▲ *Parochetus communis* Leaves clover-like, three rounded leaflets together. Growth prostrate. Flowers vivid blue like tiny sweet peas, having an erect fan-like petal behind a protruding pouch, borne singly.

▲ *Lithospermum oleifolium* Leaves elliptic, grey/green, hairy, silky on back, on wiry stems forming low hummocks. Flowers in terminal clusters several together. Tubular with five bluntly-pointed sky blue petals from pinkish buds; style prominent.

◄ *Nierembergia caerulea* (Syn. *N. hippomanica*) Leaves narrow and thread-like. Bushy tuft, with relatively large flowers. Flowers deep violet blue, shallow funnel-shaped and flared into five petals at mouth. Central yellow eye.

151

ALPINES

PURPLE & LILAC
Small Flowers:
Small Plants

▲ *Aubrieta deltoides* cultivars Leaves small, numerous, oval, toothed, forming spreading cushions. Flowers numerous with four separate petals, rounded. Wide range of colour shades, purple lavender, red.

▲ *Campanula portenschlagiana* (Syn. *C. muralis*) Leaves deep green, kidney-shaped to rounded, toothed, on slender stalks. Growth mat- or hummock-forming. Flowers numerous, bell-shaped with five triangular lobes. Blue/purple.

▶ *Aster alpinus* (Alpine Aster) Leaves spoon-shaped, coming directly from the ground and oval, pointed smaller ones along the stem. Flowers daisy-like, usually lilac with golden yellow central disc. White and pink forms occur.

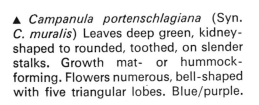

▲ *Gentiana stragulata* Leaves, oval, shiny with rounded tips. Plant tufted. Flowers long, tubular, narrowing at mouth before opening flat into five-pointed pale blue lobes, tube darker purple.

▲ *Campanula raineri* Leaves grey/green somewhat hairy, almost stemless, small, oval, toothed. Plant tufted. Flowers carried singly, relatively large, up-turned bells with five shallow, oval lobes. Light blue.

▼ *Haberlea ferdinandi-coburgii* Leaves in basal rosettes, dark green, spoon-shaped, edges notched. Flowers three or four together, on long stalks, tubular with flared mouths of five lobes, three lower ones enlarged.

▲ *Campanula fragilis* Leaves rounded to kidney-shaped, stalked, sometimes hairy, toothed. Tufted growth with arching stems. Flowers wide bell-like, with five points spreading like a star. Central style.

153

▲ *Mazus reptans* Leaves small, oval, mid-green, toothed edges. Plant makes a flat mat. Flowers numerous, comparatively large, like miniature flattened snapdragons, tubular with closed mouth surrounded by lobed lips. Blue-purple lower lip flecked with gold.

▲ *Edraianthus serpyllifolius major* (Syn. *Wahlenbergia serpyllifolia*) Leaves deep green, narrow, oval, pointed. Mat-forming. Flowers comparatively large, solitary, upturned bells of imperial purple, with five oval recurved lobes.

▶ *Haberlea rhodopensis* Leaves in a rosette, spoon-shaped, hairy, green, edges toothed. Flowers several together, tubular with flared mouths of five lobes, three lower ones enlarged. Lilac/mauve, deeper at throat. There is a white-flowered form.

▲ *Phyteuma comosum* Plant tufted. Leaves rounded to oval, glossy, bright green, toothed. Clusters of flask-shaped flowers with long thread-like protruding styles. Pink to purplish-mauve.

▼ *Thymus serpyllum* (Syn. *T. drucei*) (Thyme) Plant aromatic. Leaves small, oval, dark green, sometimes hairy. Growth creeping, carpeting with thread-like branches. Clusters of tiny flowers.

▼ *Phlox subulata* (Moss Phlox) Leaves long, narrow, rather stiff in spreading mats. Flowers very numerous above foliage in wide colour range (cultivars) from deep purple to flesh pink. Five notched widely spread petals atop a tiny tube. Darker eye.

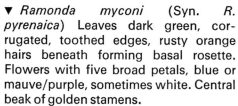

▲ *Soldanella montana* (Blue Moonwort) Leaves dark green, round, slightly toothed. Flowers nodding, carried on stiff stems, three to eight together, lavender, bell-shaped. Numerous narrow petals, fringed for more than half their length.

▼ *Ramonda myconi* (Syn. *R. pyrenaica*) Leaves dark green, corrugated, toothed edges, rusty orange hairs beneath forming basal rosette. Flowers with five broad petals, blue or mauve/purple, sometimes white. Central beak of golden stamens.

▲ *Ramonda nathaliae* Leaves bright green, glossy, oval, corrugated, hairy round edges, forming basal rosette. Flowers carried in threes cup-shaped. Four or five broad petals, lavender blue, with beak of orange/yellow stamens.

FLOWERING TREES

and woody climbers
PINK
Small Flowers: Medium Plants

A tree is a woody plant with stems that persists from year to year, usually with a single trunk. They can be deciduous or evergreen. Conebearing trees are excluded from this book because they cannot be identified from the flowers. Woody climbers are scrambling or climbing woody plants.

▲ *Crataegus laevigata* (Syn. *oxycantha*) 'Paul's Scarlet' (Pink Hawthorn, Pink May) Leaves oval, deeply lobed, shining, dark green. Growth, small and thorny. Flowers small, cup-shaped, doubled. Petals crowded in flattish clusters.

▼ *Prunus persica* 'Clara Meyer' (Double Flowering Peach) Leaves (appearing after flowers), narrow, pointed, willow-like, mid-green. Growth bushy. Flowers borne in small clusters close to bare wood, cup-shaped, double, clear pink.

▲ *Malus domestica* (Orchard Apple) Leaves broad, oval. Growth woody. Flowers white, deeply flushed pink. Buds crimson. Five cupped petals, borne in rounded clusters. Stamens yellow.

Prunus X sargentii (Sargent's Cherry) Leaves appear after flowers, bronze when young, oval pointed. Growth rounded, like small tree. Flowers with five rounded clear-pink petals. Cluster of pink stamens. Buds crimson/pink.

▼ *Prunus triloba* (Double Flowering Almond) Leaves three-lobed with coarsely toothed edge. Growth medium to large. Flowers double, pale pink like rosettes, borne in clusters held close to branches.

▼ *Prunus subhirtella* 'Pendula' (Weeping Spring Cherry) Leaves oval, somewhat glossy. Growth slender, pendulous or weeping. Flowers profuse but small, pale pink, five-petalled, carried close to stems, creating hanging ribbons of growth.

PINK
Medium Flowers: Medium Plants

▼ *Clematis X jackmanii* 'Comtesse de Bouchard' Leaves divided into several (usually three) oblong, pointed leaflets. Growth slender, climbing. Flowers with six petals, soft rose pink, darker at edges, ribbed. Boss of golden stamens.

▲ *Clematis montana* 'Rubens' Leaves divided into several oval, pointed, leaflets, bronzed when young. Growth rampant, scrambling. Flowers pale pink. Four petals. Central boss of golden stamens, borne in great profusion.

▼ *Lonicera X americana* Leaves elliptical to oval. Growth vigorous. A climber. Flowers long, tubular, white, ageing to deep yellow stained with purple. Stamens prominent, fragrant. Borne in abundant terminal clusters.

▲ *Prunus serrulata* 'Kanzan' (Japanese Flowering Cherry) Leaves coppery red when young, oval, pointed. Growth upright. Flowers semi-double rosettes. Petals notched, overlapping, purple/pink borne in profusion.

◄ *Rosa* 'May Queen' (Wichuriana Rambler Rose) Leaves divided into several glossy, oval, pointed leaflets. Growth slender, flexible, thorny, climbing. Flowers completely double, cups filled with overlapping lilac/pink petals. Fresh apple fragrance.

► *Rosa* 'Mme Grégoire Staechelin' (Climbing Hybrid Tea Rose) Leaves composed of several oval, rich green leaflets. Growth arching. A woody climber. Flowers fragrant, clear pink, fully double. Petals overlapping, fill goblet shaped flowers. A very prolific flowerer.

PINK
Large Flowers: Small Plants

▶ *Clematis* 'Ville de Lyon' (Hybrid Clematis) Leaves divided into several oval, pointed leaflets. Growth slender, stems burnished. A climber. Flowers flat, madder pink. Six broad-pointed petals, central rib. Boss of yellow stamens, upstanding solitary.

PINK
Large Flowers: Medium Plants

▶ *Magnolia X soulangiana* 'Rustica Rubra' Leaves oval with prominent centre rib, mid-green. Growth like large bush or small spreading tree. Flowers rich rose red suffused with cream, deeper at base, upstanding, goblet-shaped.

FLOWERING TREES

and woody climbers

RED
Small Flowers:
Medium Plants

◀ *Crinodendron hookerianum* (Syn. *Tricuspidaria lanceolatum*) (Lantern Tree) Leaves evergreen, narrow, pointed, somewhat glossy, central rib prominent. Growth dense. Flowers crimson, numerous, borne in long stalked hanging lanterns.

RED
Medium Flowers:
Medium Plants

◀ *Lonicera sempervirens* (Trumpet vine or honeysuckle) Leaves grey/green, oval. Growth twining. A climber. Flowers tubular, rich fire red, paler within, borne in terminal clusters.

RED
Medium Flowers:
Tall Plants

◀ *Aesculus X carnea* (Red Horse Chestnut) Leaves hand-shaped, composed of five to seven large oval leaflets. Growth tree-like. Flowers rose pink in upstanding spires with prominent stamens.

RED
Large Flowers:
Medium Plants

◀ *Magnolia liliflora* 'Nigra' Leaves broad, oval, shining, dark green above pale beneath. Growth large, shrubby and spreading. Flowers upright like large slender tulips. Red/purple in bud, paler within.

FLOWERING TREES

and woody climbers

ORANGE & YELLOW
Small Flowers:
Medium Plants

▲ *Clematis rehderiana* Leaves divided into several oval leaflets. Growth vigorous. A climber. Flowers borne in terminal sprays, nodding primrose yellow bells with curled back petal tips. Primrose fragrance.

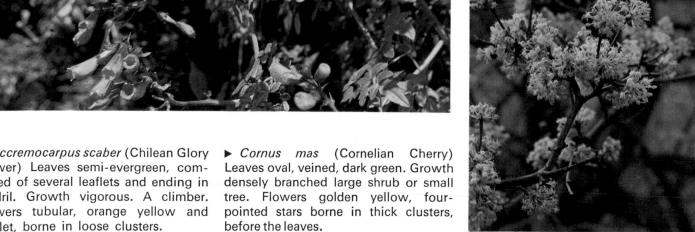

▲ *Eccremocarpus scaber* (Chilean Glory Flower) Leaves semi-evergreen, composed of several leaflets and ending in tendril. Growth vigorous. A climber. Flowers tubular, orange yellow and scarlet, borne in loose clusters.

▶ *Cornus mas* (Cornelian Cherry) Leaves oval, veined, dark green. Growth densely branched large shrub or small tree. Flowers golden yellow, four-pointed stars borne in thick clusters, before the leaves.

▲ *Koelreutia paniculata* Goldenrain Tree, Pride of India) Leaves composed of nine to fifteen oval, pointed leaflets in two rows. Growth broad, like small tree. Flowers small, golden yellow, borne in loose plume-like sprays.

▼ *Salix caprea* (Goat Willow, Great Sallow) Leaves oval, grey/green and hairy beneath. Growth large, bushy, like small tree. Flowers cone-shaped golden catkins on bare stems (silver, downy, bud-shaped catkins, when young).

▲ *Laburnum X vossi* (Hybrid Golden Rain, Voss, Laburnum) Leaves composed of three dull green, oval leaflets. Growth broad, like small tree. Flowers buttercup yellow, sweet-pea-like, borne in long drooping chains.

ORANGE & YELLOW
Medium Flowers: Medium Plants

▲ *Lonicera X tellmanniana* Leaves oval, sometimes stem-clasping. Growth vigorous. A climber. Flowers tubular with coppery-orange, wide-flaring mouth, upper lip three-lobed, lower one narrow and horizontal. Stamens protrude. Borne in large terminal clusters.

▲ *Rosa X 'Mermaid'* (Climbing Rose) Leaves divided into several glossy, oval, slightly-toothed leaflets. Growth vigorous. A climber. Flowers single, flat on maturity. Petals roll or twist, sulphur yellow. Amber stamens make up delicate central boss.

▲ *Clematis orientalis* Leaves divided into several elliptical leaflets, dainty, fern-like. Growth vigorous. A climber. Flowers fragrant, buttercup yellow, solitary, nodding. Four-pointed thick-textured petals like sun hats above black/gold sheaf of stamens.

ORANGE & YELLOW
Medium Flowers: Tall Plants

▶ *Lonicera hildebrandiana* (Giant Honeysuckle) Leaves evergreen, oval, tapering, rich green. Growth very vigorous. A climber. Flowers fragrant, very long, curved, tubular, several together with flaring mouth. White turning to beige/yellow.

165

FLOWERING TREES

and woody climbers

WHITE, GREEN & CREAM

Small Flowers: Small Plants

▲ *Chionanthus virginicus* (Fringe Tree) Leaves elliptic to oval, pointed. Growth like large shrub or small tree with greyish bark. Flowers white. Four or five narrow strap-shaped petals in dense fluffy clusters. Fragrant.

◀ *Pieris formosa forrestii* Leaves evergreen, elliptic to oval with central vein, glossy. Young foliage cardinal red. Growth dense. Flowers slightly fragrant with white bells in pendent or arching clusters.

▶ *Pieris japonica* (Syn. *Andromeda japonica*) Leaves evergreen, elliptical, with central vein, glossy, burnished red or copper when young. Growth dense. Flowers waxy white bells borne in drooping clusters.

WHITE, GREEN & CREAM
Small Flowers: Medium Plants

▶ *Crataegus X lavallei* Leaves oval to triangular in outline, toothed, glossy. Growth dense, somewhat spiny. Flowers fragrant. Five cup-shaped petals surround a cluster of cream stamens.

▲ *Humulus lupulus* 'Aureus' (Golden Hop) Leaves rough, heart-shaped, pointed, deeply veined, toothed, golden green. Growth twining. A climber. Flowers insignificant, greenish-yellow. Fruits cone-like, hanging in clusters (hops).

▼ *Crataegus laevigata* (Syn. *C. oxycantha*) (Hawthorn) Leaves oval, shallowly-lobed, glossy. Growth dense, somewhat spiny. Flowers heavy, almond-fragrant, profuse. Five-cupped white petals enfold central cluster of stamens. Flowers borne in great abundance.

▲ *Hedera helix* 'Variegata' (Common Ivy) Leaves evergreen, broad oval, three to five-lobed, pointed, bright green/grey, margins cream. Growth vigorous. A climber. Flowers small, green, several in a globular head.

▼ *Arbutus unedo* (Killarney Strawberry Tree) Leaves evergreen, elliptic to oval. Gnarled bark, copper/bronze shredding. Flowers white, like pendulous bells borne in groups on reddish stalks.

◄ *Myoporum laetum* (Ngaio) Leaves evergreen, elliptic to oval, leathery with translucent spots. Growth bushy. Flowers small, white, spotted with purple. Five pointed flaring petals borne in clusters close to stems.

▼ *Pyrancantha crenulata* 'Rogersiana' (Firethorn) Leaves evergreen, oval, toothed. Growth dense, thorny. Flowers small. Five cream petals, massed into rounded heads and borne in profusion.

▼ *Drimys winteri* (Winter Bark) Leaves elliptical, glossy, evergreen, leathery, blue/white beneath. Growth like large shrub or narrow tree. Flowers white, fragrant, bowl-shaped, pendent.

▲ *Sorbus aucuparia* (Rowan, Mountain Ash) Leaves divided into two rows of elliptical leaflets. Growth like small tree. Flowers small, numerous, in loose flattish heads, cream/white, appearing fluffy with protruding stamens.

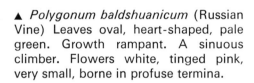

▲ *Prunus spinosa* (Sloe, Blackthorn) Leaves oval, small. Growth, dense and shrubby or, less commonly, like small tree. Bark dark. Branches spiny. Flowers white, appearing fluffy from numerous prominent stamens. Five separate petals, borne close to stems before leaves.

▲ *Polygonum baldshuanicum* (Russian Vine) Leaves oval, heart-shaped, pale green. Growth rampant. A sinuous climber. Flowers white, tinged pink, very small, borne in profuse termina.

◀ *Prunus avium* 'Plena' (Syn. 'Multiplex') (Double Gean, Mazzard, Wild Cherry) Leaves oval, fresh green, prominently veined. Growth small to medium tree-like. Bark grey, reddish later. Flowers cup-shaped, in clusters.

▲ *Sorbus aria* (Whitebeam) Leaves oval, dusty white when young, green later but remaining vividly white beneath. Growth compact, round-headed tree. Flowers small, cream, in flat heads. Five petals.

◄ *Solanum jasminoides* 'Album' (Potato Vine) Leaves oval, tapering, glossy, thin. Growth slender. A vigorous climber. Flowers like starry cups. Five broad petals. Yellow central 'beak' of stamens.

▼ *Prunus laurocerasus* (Cherry Laurel, Laurel) Leaves evergreen, shining, elliptical to long, central vein, prominent. Growth wide spreading, like large shrub or small tree. Flowers dull white, starry, borne in upstanding candle-like spikes.

WHITE, GREEN & CREAM
Small Flowers: Tall Plants

▶ *Actinidia kolomikta* Leaves broad, oval, pointed, tri-coloured; green, creamy white and pink. Growth slender. A climber. Flowers slightly fragrant, white, bowl-shaped, usually rather hidden by foliage.

WHITE, GREEN & CREAM
Large Flowers: Medium Plants

▶ *Magnolia sargentiana* (Sargent's Magnolia) Leaves oval, broad, leathery. Growth upright like medium sized tree. Flowers like pink water lilies, upstanding on bare branches.

▼ *Magnolia obovata* Leaves oval, broader at the tip, pale to mid-green. Flowers bowl-shaped, composed of six to nine oval cream petals. Each petal terminates in a tiny spike.

▼ *Magnolia sieboldii* Leaves oval, pale green. Flowers somewhat nodding at tips of twigs, pure white with a boss of crimson stamens. Usually six petals.

▼ *Magnolia wilsoni* (Wilson's Magnolia) Leaves elliptic to lance-shaped. Growth spreading, like shrubby tree. Flowers pendulous, white, bowl-shaped with central golden candle.

WHITE, GREEN & CREAM
Large Flowers: Tall Plants

▶ *Liriodendron tulipifera* (Tulip Tree)
Leaves rectangular, somewhat saddle-shaped with four-pointed lobes, distinctive. Growth upright like large tree. Flowers jade-green and orange, cup-shaped, upstanding and filled with straw-like yellow stamens.

FLOWERING TREES

and woody climbers
PURPLE &
LILAC
Medium Flowers:
Medium Plants

▲ *Clematis macropetala* Leaves divided into several oval, pointed, leaflets. Growth slender. A climber. Flowers violet with pendulous bells. Petals long and pointed. Lavender petal-like segments inside with cream stamens.

▶ *Clematis* 'Ap-pare' (Large-flowered Clematis) Leaves mid-green, divided into several oval, pointed, leaflets. Growth slender. A climber. Flowers flat with six broad-pointed petals, lavender shot with blue, ribbed. Pistil and stamens forming central boss of plum/ purple, black and cream, very striking.

▶ *Solanum crispum* Leaves oval, somewhat downy. Growth vigorous. A scrambling shrub. Flowers blue/purple, five-pointed star with central golden 'beak' of stamens. Slightly fragrant.

◀ *Wisteria floribunda* (Japanese Wisteria) Leaves divided into two rows of elliptical, pointed leaflets. Growth vigorous. A woody climber. Flowers small, fragrant, violet and purple, sweet pea-like in long hanging tails.

PURPLE & LILAC
Small Flowers: Medium Plants

▲ *Clematis.* 'Mrs Cholmondeley' Leaves divided into three or more oval, pointed, leaflets. Growth vigorous. A climber. Flowers flat with six broad pointed petals, lilac, overlaid blue/purple. Central boss of cream spikey stamens.

▲ *Clematis X jackmanii* Leaves divided into three or more oval, pointed, leaflets on slender stems. Growth vigorous. A climber. Flowers flat with four large broad petals. Petals pointed, rich purple with central ridges suffused magenta. Central boss of cream spikey stamens.

AQUATICS

PINK
Small Flowers: Small Plants

An aquatic is a plant which lives partially or wholly in water or very boggy conditions. The growth is either trailing and lax under water or upright and held well above the water surface. Many are vigorous and spread rapidly.

▶ *Epipactus palustris* (Marsh Helleborine) Leaves strap-shaped, dull green and enclosing stem at base. Flowers in loose spike. Three inner petals, white, strongly suffused with creamy pink, within three darker greenish-red outer petals. Nodding.

PINK
Small Flowers: Medium Plants

▶ *Primula pulverulenta* Leaves long, oval, crinkled, pale green, in basal rosette. Flowers claret, borne in ruffs or whorls at intervals along white mealy stem and at top. Primrose shaped.

PINK
Large Flowers: Medium Plants

▶ *Nymphaea odorata* 'William Shaw' (Shaw's Waterlily) Leaves circular, floating. Flowers stand above water, cup-shaped, finally opening out flat and starry. Usually a pinkish cream colour.

AQUATICS

RED
Small Flowers: Small Plants

▶ *Pyrola asarifolia* (Wintergreen) Leaves thin, leathery, heart-shaped, shining. Flowers pendent bells, opening widely in very loose spires at top of red stem. Thriving only in damp woodland or boggy conditions.

RED
Small Flowers:
Medium Plants

▶ *Schrophularia aquatica* 'Variegata' (Variegated Water Figwort) Leaves the main feature of the plant, in pairs along stem, oval, round-toothed, dark green broadly margined with cream. Flowers small red-brown helmets carried in clusters near top of rigid four sided stem.

RED
Large Flowers:
Medium Plants

▶ *Nymphaea* 'James Brydon' (Water-lily) Leaves rounded, leathery, glossy, reddish when young, green later, on long trailing stems, floating on water surface. Flowers cup-shaped, petals wide spreading, overlapping, triangular, deep pink to sealing wax red.

AQUATICS

ORANGE & YELLOW
Small Flowers: Small Plants

► *Mimulus luteus* (Monkey Musk). Leaves heart-shaped, stem-clasping, smooth. Flowers golden yellow, borne above foliage, with two-lipped trumpets – the upper small one two-lobed, the lower large one four-lobed. Often marked with reddish spots.

ORANGE & YELLOW
Small Flowers: Medium Plants

► *Caltha palustris* 'Plena' (Double Marsh Marigold) Leaves rounded, slightly toothed, deep green, held above surface of mud or shallow water. Flowers golden yellow pom-poms freely borne above the leaves.

► *Primula florindae* (Giant Himalayan Cowslip) Leaves oval, edges waved and toothed in ground-hugging clusters. Flowers well above foliage in large clustered heads of long spreading or pendulous bells. Stalks rise from the top of the stem. Sulphur yellow, sometimes red flushed.

ORANGE & YELLOW
Large Flowers: Medium Plants

▶ *Nuphar lutea* (Brandy Bottle, Yellow Waterlily) Leaves oval, deeply heart-shaped, mid green, glossy and floating. Flowers solitary, held well above water on stout stem, golden yellow, cup-shaped and filled with stamens. Fruit like a green flask. Grows in deep water.

AQUATICS

WHITE, GREEN & CREAM
Small Flowers: Medium Plants

▶ *Peltandra virginica* (Green Arrow Arum) Leaves arrow-shaped with upright stems above bog or water. Flowers in rod-like spike enclosed in tightly rolled green petal-like sheath (spathe).

▲ *Stratiotes aloides* (Water Soldier) Leaves sword-like, tough with serrated edges, borne in a rosette upstanding from the water at flowering time, sinking later. Flowers three-petalled, white, solitary, carried low amongst the leaves.

▲ *Sagittaria sagittifolia* (Arrowhead) Leaves like the head of an arrow or spear, long, pointed, light green, upstanding. Flowers three-petalled, white with brown stamens at centre. In small whorls at top of thick upright stems.

◄ *Ranunculus aquatilis* Leaves round-lobed, thread-like, floating on trailing stems in water. Flowers upstanding on brownish pink hollow stems, solitary, white with central golden boss of stamens. Five separate petals.

WHITE, GREEN & CREAM
Small Flowers: Tall Plants

▶ *Peltiphyllum peltatum* (Umbrella plant) Leaves circular, edges indented, large umbrella-like. Flowers borne in large domed head on tall thick stalk before leaves. Five petals, rounded and spaced with central red stigma.

WHITE, GREEN & CREAM
Large Flowers: Medium Plants

▶ *Nymphaea* 'Lactaea' (Hybrid White Waterlily) Leaves circular, glossy on long trailing stems, floating on water surface. Flowers cup-shaped, petals overlapping pointed. Starry apricot tinted at first, becoming pure white.

AQUATICS

PURPLE & LILAC
Small Flowers: Medium Plants

▶ *Pontederia cordata* (Pickerel Weed) Leaves long, heart-shaped, pointed, graceful, shining green and upstanding above water or bog. Flowers small and numerous borne in conical spikes at the ends of upright stalks. Purple/blue.

SHRUBS

PINK
Small Flowers: Small Plants

Shrubs are plants in which the top growth is woody and persists year after year, but does not form a central trunk. The leaves may fall at the end of the season (deciduous) or may remain through the winter (evergreen). Shrubs can vary in size, form and habit and the flowers can also vary widely. Woody plants of less than 8 cm in height, for the purpose of this book, are included in the section on Alpines.

▲ *Gaultheria shallon* (Salal) Leaves oval, broad, pointed, leathery, evergreen. Growth dense. Flowers pale pink to white, urn-shaped, borne in loose arching spikes. Globular edible black fruit.

◄ *Calluna vulgaris* (Ling, Heather) Leaves small, scale-like, clothing the twiggy stems thickly, evergreen. Flowers like minute rounded bells, numerous, carried in spikes. Low bushy growth.

► *Erica cinerea* 'Golden hue' (Golden-leaved Bell Heather) Leaves very small, needle-shaped, golden green turning red in winter, evergreen. Flowers tubular bells. Stamens protrude, numerous, carried in spikes at the ends of the branches.

► *Helianthemum* 'Wisley Pink' (Sun Rose, Rock Rose) Leaves long and narrow, grey/green with strong central vein, evergreen. Growth twiggy and matted. Flowers plentiful, five-petalled, clear shell pink. Central yellow boss of stamens.

▼ *Phyllodoce empetriformis* Leaves needle-like, small, clustered close to twiggy stems. Flowers bell-shaped, with frilled rims. Style protruding like a 'clapper'. Deep pink, borne in long clusters.

▼ *Rosa* 'Pixie' (Miniature Rose) Leaves usually made up of five oval, shining leaflets. Growth bushy, woody. Flowers double. Petals numerous and full, opening almost flat. Buds deeper pink than flowers.

185

▲ *Spiraea X bumalda* 'Anthony Waterer' Leaves long, narrow, pointed and toothed. Growth twiggy, erect. Terminal leaves often with some cream and pink variegation. Flowers small with five deep pink petals, carried in flat terminal heads.

▲ *Skimmia rubella* (Syn. *S. reevesiana* 'Rubella') Leaves leathery, lance-shaped, pointed, evergreen, aromatic when crushed. Growth bushy and rounded. Flowers borne in conical clustered heads. Four petals, opening from narrow tube. Buds deep pink. Oval red fruits.

◀ *Vaccinium vitis-idaea* (Cowberry, Mountain Cranberry) Leaves small, broadly oval, shining, evergreen, forming dense mat. Growth creeping. Pink urn-shaped flowers borne in hanging clusters, four or five together. Dark red round berries.

PINK
Small Flowers: Medium Plants

▼ *Abelia X grandiflora* Leaves oval, shining, pointed, semi-evergreen. Growth slender and spreading. Deep pink, long, tubular flowers flaring at tips into five segments. Borne in clusters. Fragrant.

▼ *Cotinus coggygria* (Syn. *Rhus cotinus*) (Smoke Bush or Tree) Leaves light green becoming red in autumn, oval, very smooth. Growth rounded. Flowers flesh pink turning grey later, in foamy pyramidal clusters above the foliage.

▲ *Cotoneaster horizontalis* Leaves small, broadly oval, pointed, somewhat shining. Growth in distinctive flat herringbone formation. Flowers pink, rounded in bud. Five petals, numerous, borne in leaf axils. Abundant round red berries.

▶ *Clerodendron bungei* (Syn. *C. foetidum*) Leaves heart-shaped, pointed, clothed with violet hairs, fetid when crushed. Flowers in tightly packed rounded heads. Five strap-shaped petals with very long protruding stamens. Fragrant. Deep rose pink.

◄ *Cytisus purpureus* (Purple Broom) Leaves divided into three small oval leaflets. Growth arching, graceful. Flowers plentiful, like miniature sweet peas borne along branches towards ends. Lilac pink and cyclamen.

► *Cercis siliquastrum* (Judas Tree) Leaves rounded, somewhat pointed at tips, pale green at first becoming darker. Growth spreading. Flowers borne in dense clusters on bare wood before leaves, like small sweet peas, bright rosy-purple.

▲ *Elsholtzia stauntonii* Leaves lance shaped, smelling of mint when crushed, green above, paler beneath. Growth upright. Flowers borne in upstanding spikes, tubular and numerous, pinkish-mauve. Fluffy appearance.

▲ *Escallonia* 'Peach Blossom' Leaves thick, shining, oval, toothed, evergreen. Growth dense, bushy. Flowers numerous, bright pink, paler within, bell-shaped with five petals opening wider at mouth. Borne in compact clusters.

▶ *Deutzia* 'Magician' Leaves long, tapering to point, bright green. Growth upright. Flowers clustered along previous season's stem, rose pink and star-like with five broad pointed petals, darker stripe on back.

▲ *Prunus tenella* 'Fire Hill' (Syn. *P. gessleriana*) (Dwarf Russian Almond) Leaves long oval, smooth, bright green and glossy. Growth upright. Flowers rosy-crimson, with five starry petals, borne in profusion along bare branches before the leaves.

▶ *Kolkwitzia amabilis* (Beauty Bush) Leaves oval, rough, hairy, toothed. Flowers candy pink, funnel-shaped with five-lobed rim, mouth resembling a foxglove, throats yellow. Borne in dense clusters.

▲ *Weigela florida* Leaves oval, wrinkled pointed, entire (occasionally purple or variegated). Growth shrubby. Flowers trumpet-shaped with long tube behind, opening to five wide lobes. Rose pink, paler within.

▶ *Spiraea salicifolia* (Bridewort) Leaves long, narrow, pointed, toothed, somewhat like willow leaves. Growth erect. Flowers pale pink, small, borne in dense oblong spikes, fluffy because of protruding anthers.

◄ *Rubus ulmifolius* 'Bellidiflorus' (Daisy-flowered Bramble) Leaves made up of three to five pointed toothed leaflets, pale beneath dark green above. Growth scrambling with thorns. Flowers fully double, rose pink like pom-poms, borne in terminal clusters.

▲ *Dais cotinifolia* Leaves, oval, dark green, paler beneath. Growth dense and bushy. Flower-heads rounded and flattened. Flowers long and tubular opening to five strap-shaped lobes, pale lilac.

▼ *Viburnum tinus* (Laurustinus) Leaves dark green oval to oblong, evergreen. Growth dense, bushy. Flowers borne in flat clusters. Buds deep pink, opening white, somewhat fragrant.

► *Notospartium carmicheliae* (New Zealand Pink Broom) Leaves scale-like, sparse, appearing leafless. Growth graceful. Flowers borne in short sprays along bare arching green branches. Soft mauve-pink, sweet-pea-like. Upper fan petal folded.

▼ *Kalmia latifolia* 'Brilliant' (Calico Bush) Leaves large, smooth, evergreen, long, narrow. Growth dense. Flowers borne in bold clusters. Buds like icing sugar 'stars'. When open, bowl-shaped. Deep pink, waxy.

▼ *Kalmia latifolia* (Calico Bush) Leaves large, smooth, evergreen, long, narrow. Growth dense. Flowers borne in bold clusters. Buds like icing sugar 'stars'. When open, bowl-shaped. Shell pink, waxy.

PINK
Medium Flowers: Small Plants

▶ *Rhododendron williamsianum* Leaves small, round to heart-shaped, dark green. Growth spreading. Flowers like bells opening to five lobes at mouth. Buds red, fading to soft pink as they open.

PINK
Medium Flowers: Medium Plants

◀ *Cistus X purpureus* (Sun Rose) Leaves long, narrow, pointed, grey/green. Growth well-rounded and upright. Flowers opening singly in succession. Five crumpled, broad, madder pink petals with maroon patch at base. Boss of golden stamens.

▼ *Hibiscus* 'The President' Leaves broad, shining, deeply lobed, jagged. Flowers like slightly twisted funnel. Five rounded petals, pale pink flushed purple at the base, etched with darker veins. Protruding cluster of stamens like bottle brush.

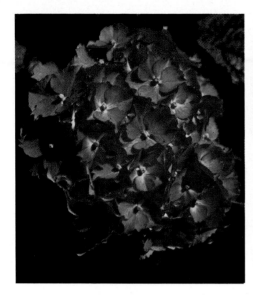

▲ *Hydrangea macrophylla* 'Hamburg' (Common Hydrangea) Leaves broadly oval, pointed, toothed. Growth rounded. Flowers in large globular heads, deep rose pink. Petals with scalloped edges, slightly paler at centre.

▶ *Rosa gallica* 'Versicolor' (Syn. 'Rosa Mundi') (York and Lancaster Rose) Leaves made up of three to five oval, dark green leaflets. Growth bushy and upright. Flowers semi-double. Petals overlap, crimson, striped with pink or white. Central boss of golden stamens.

▼ *Hydrangea macrophylla* 'Mariesii' (Lace-cap Hydrangea) Leaves broadly oval, pointed, toothed. Growth bushy. Flowers carried in wide flat terminal heads. Outer ones sterile, large, shell pink, four-petalled, surrounding head of tiny deeper-coloured flowers.

▼ *Rosa* 'Henri Martin' (Moss Rose) Leaves made up of small, rounded, smooth, toothed leaflets. Growth bristly. Flowers heavy and double. Petals wavy, bright crimson-pink. Buds covered with 'mossy' glands.

195

▲ *Rosa* 'Zephirine Drouhin' (Bourbon Rose) Leaves made up of oval, pointed, light green leaflets. Growth bushy or climbing, thornless. Flowers semi-double. Petals overlap and are rolled back over each other, bright pink.

▲ *Rosa* 'Pink Supreme' (Hybrid Tea Rose) Leaves made up of three or more oval, smooth, toothed, glossy, light green leaflets. Growth vigorous, bushy and thorny. Flowers double, posy-shaped. Petals overlap and curve outward, bright pink, fragrant.

▶ *Rosa* 'Louise Odier' (Bourbon Rose) Leaves made up of three or more smooth, finely-toothed leaflets. Growth bushy, thornless. Flowers heavy, fully double. Petals overlap, crowded. Deep rose pink.

▼ *Rosa* 'Queen Elizabeth' (Floribunda Rose) Leaves made up of several shining, smooth, toothed leaflets. Growth vigorous, erect and thorny. Flowers fully double, soft clear pink, carried in upright sprays.

PINK
Medium Flowers: Tall Plants

▼ *Rhododendron* 'Mermaid' (Rhododendron) Leaves large, evergreen, oval, clustered like collar behind flower head. Growth upright. Flowers borne in compact clusters, large and trumpet-shaped, with rose pink five-lobed mouth.

▶ *Rhododendron arboreum* (Tree Rhododendron) Leaves long, smooth, evergreen, dark green above, buff beneath. Flowers borne in large cluster, trumpet-shaped, with five-lobed mouth, frilly and showy. Clear pink, speckled maroon within.

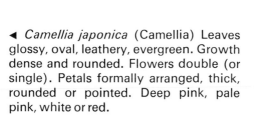

◀ *Camellia japonica* (Camellia) Leaves glossy, oval, leathery, evergreen. Growth dense and rounded. Flowers double (or single). Petals formally arranged, thick, rounded or pointed. Deep pink, pale pink, white or red.

SHRUBS
RED
Small Flowers: Small Plants

▲ *Rosa* 'Red Imp' (Miniature Rose) Leaves divided into several oval, pointed, shining leaflets. Growth bushy with prickles. Flowers double, like crimson pom-poms on simply-branched stems.

▲ *Helianthemum* 'Beech Park Scarlet' (Rock Rose, Sun Rose) Leaves sage green, small, narrowly oval. Growth twiggy, spreading in small terminal clusters. Five rounded red petals held flat with small central boss of stamens.

▼ *Rhododendron* 'Hinodegirii' (Japanese Kurume Azalea) Leaves small, glossy, oval and plentiful. Growth bushy. Crimson flowers, wide funnel-shaped, flaring into five-lobed mouth, borne profusely almost smothering plant. Stamens protrude.

▼ *Sarmentia repens* Leaves small, oval, evergreen. Growth, creeping, mat-forming. Flowers red, like Grecian urns, with a flared lobed mouth. Long red stamens protrude.

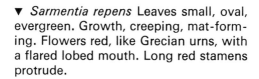

RED
Small Flowers:
Medium Plants

◀ *Cytisus X burkwoodii* (Burkwood's Broom) Leaves very small, oval, soon falling, borne along stem. Growth arching plumes of green stems. Flowers showy, very plentiful, in plumes and wands. Like miniature sweet-peas, velvety crimson, edged with yellow.

▼ *Rhus typhina* (Stag's Horn, Sumach) Leaves divided into lance-shaped leaflets, arranged in pairs. Growth erect, branched like stags horns. Flowers small, in erect cone-line clusters, above foliage. Crimson/brown reddening with age.

◄ *Diplacus glutinosus* (Californian Shrubby Mimulus) Leaves long narrow and pointed. Growth spreading and bushy. Flowers showy, funnel-like, with five flared scalloped lobes. Splashed with darker tones, varying from buff yellow to mahogany red.

► *Salvia grahamii* Leaves oval, blunt, small. Growth open and bushy. Flowers scarlet, tubular, borne in small terminal spikes with inflated open mouth, lower lip fan-like.

◄ *Ribes speciosum* Leaves rounded, deeply three-lobed. Growth arching, thorny. Tubular, narrow, rectangular, shining sealing wax red flowers dangle like lanterns beneath branches. Thread-like stamens protrude.

► *Ribes sanguineum* (Flowering Currant) Leaves rounded three to five-lobed, toothed, prominently veined. Growth erect, open and bushy. Flowers arranged in hanging clusters. Five petals flaring, cherry red.

RED
Medium Flowers: Medium Plants

▶ *Fuchsia* 'Mrs Popple' Leaves oval, somewhat shining, toothed, mid-ribs often red. Growth low, arching open shrub. Flowers pendulous on red stems. Purple bells, backed by four-pointed red stars. Long red stamens protrude.

▲ *Rhododendron cinnabarinum roylei*
Leaves oval, metallic, evergreen. Growth
erect and bushy with slender branches.
Flowers like pendulous narrow bells,
vermillion, paler within, in groups of five
to eight.

▲ *Rosa moyesii* Leaves divided into
several pairs of oval, toothed, leaflets.
Growth large. Purplish stems with
prickles. Flowers saucer-shaped, blood
red or crimson. Five broad notched
petals.

▲ *Chaenomeles speciosa* (Syn. *C. lagenaria*) (Japanese Quince, Japonica). Leaves oval to oblong, glossy. Growth woody, stiff. Flowers blood red, wide cup-shaped. Five broad petals with central cluster of yellow stamens. Often appearing before leaves.

▶ *Rosa* 'Ena Harkness' (Hybrid Tea Rose) Leaves composed of several oval, veined, toothed leaflets. Growth prickly. Flowers borne singly or a few together at ends of simply-branched stems, fully double, velvety crimson. Petals tightly overlap, outer ones recurving at tips.

▲ *Rosa* 'Evelyn Fison' (Floribunda Rose) Leaves composed of several oval, toothed, leaflets. Growth vigorous and prickly. Flowers in terminal clusters, fully double, frilly and rosette-like, bright scarlet, velvety.

▶ *Rosa* 'Superstar' (Hybrid Tea Rose) Leaves divided into several oval, toothed, leaflets. Growth prickly. Flowers borne singly or a few together at ends of simply-branched stems, fully double, pillar box red, outer petals recurved.

▲ *Paeonia delavayi* (Delavay's Tree Peony) Leaves divided into several long, narrow pointed, lobed leaflets. Growth sparse and open. Flowers black/crimson, like shallow bowls, filled with stamens. Borne singly or a few together.

▶ *Weigela* hybrid 'Newport Red' Leaves oval-pointed, plentiful. Growth graceful. Flowers in terminal clusters with small wide flaring trumpets with slender tubes. Mouth five wide rounded lobes, rich red. Stamens and style protrude.

SHRUBS
ORANGE & YELLOW
Small Flowers:
Small Plants

▲ *Cytisus X kewensis* Leaves narrow, oval, small and pale green. Growth spreading with long arching stems, dense. Flowers creamy yellow like miniature sweet peas. A fan-like petal behind a tight pouch or keel. Carried in profusion along stems.

▲ *Potentilla arbuscula* (Cinquefoil) Leaves small, narrowly-oval, lobed, like fingers of a hand. Branches covered with brown hairs. Growth low, erect. Flowers flat, butter yellow. Five rounded petals.

▲ *Halimium lasianthum* (Syn. *Helianthemum formosum*) Leaves grey/green, narrowly oval. Growth lax spreading. Flowers borne singly, saucer-like, golden yellow with red-purple marking at base of each of five petals.

► *Hypericum fragile* Leaves small, oval, sparse. Growth, tangled, cushion-forming. Flowers comparatively large for the plant, buttercup yellow. Five spoon-shaped petals, held flat. Prominent boss of slender yellow stamens.

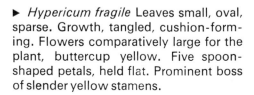

▲ *Hypericum olympicum* Leaves small, oval, grey/green, on wiry stems. Growth, sub-shrub, upright. Flowers bright yellow in clusters, very free-flowering. Five spoon-shaped petals. Central boss of long stamens. (Paler flower forms occur.)

▲ *Reinwardtia trigyna* (Syn. *R. indica,
Linum trigynum*) Leaves light green,
oval, pointed. Growth erect. Flowers
butter yellow borne in profusion, flat.
Five rounded petals opening from funnel-shaped tube, slightly overlapping,
wavy. Five stamens tucked into throat.

◄ *Salix retusa* (Blunt-leaved Willow)
Leaves small, glossy, oval to oblong.
Growth woody, prostrate. Flowers carried in small rounded catkins, male with
long stamens. Yellow.

▲ *Ulex europaeus* (Gorse, Furze, Whin)
Leaves scale-like. Stems dark green
tipped with spines. Stiff branches.
Growth dense and rigid. Flowers golden
yellow like small peas. Black fan petal
rounded and sheltering pouch or keel.

▲ *Ruta Chalepensis* (Rue, Herb of
Grace) Leaves blue/green, hairless made
up of wedge-shaped leaflets. Growth
rounded. Plant with foetid smell. Flowers
dominated by green globular centre.
Four cupped deep yellow petals. Stamens arranged alternately with them.

◄ *Santolina chamaecyparissus* (Syn. *S.
incana*) (Cotton Lavender) Leaves sil-
ver/grey, long, narrow, deeply cut,
coral-like. Aromatic. Growth compact,
evergreen. Flowers numerous in compact globular heads. Bright yellow
buttons or pom-poms.

ORANGE & YELLOW
Small Flowers: Medium Plants

▲ *Berberis darwinii* (Berberis, Barberry) Leaves dark green, glossy, evergreen, like small holly leaves. Growth arching. Flowers orange/yellow, rounded. Ovoid bells with separate petals, borne profusely in loose hanging clusters.

◄ *Chimonanthus praecox* (Syn. *C. fragrans, Calycanthus praecox*) (Wintersweet) Leaves long-oval, pointed, shiny, produced after flowers. Growth upright. Flowers cup-shaped, with waxy, large, yellow, outer petals. Smaller inner ones purple/brown. Heavily fragrant.

▶ *Colutea arborescens* (Bladder Senna) Leaves made up of five to nine small oval leaflets carried in pairs. Growth arching. Flowers bright yellow pea-shaped. Upper fan petals back pouch or keel. Followed by large purple/brown inflated pods.

▼ *Cytisus scoparius* 'Andreanus' (Common Broom) Leaves small, narrow, carried close to branches. Growth arching plumes. Flowers bright yellow and crimson maroon like miniature sweet pea flowers. Erect fan petal behind pouch or keel petals, somewhat folded. Numerous.

▼ *Cytisus battandieri* Leaves divided into three oval leaflets, green with silver silky sheen. Flowers borne in long densely clustered heads, bright yellow, sweet-pea-like. Pineapple scented.

◄ *Potentilla fruticosa* (Shrubby cinquefoil). Leaves made up of five or seven small narrow leaflets. Growth upright, dense. Flowers golden yellow, soft, saucer-shaped, freely borne with five rounded petals.

▼ *Mahonia japonica* Leaves large, polished, made up of five to nine oblong, spiny leaflets. Growth compact. Flowers lemon yellow bells with outer fringe of petals, borne in long drooping sprays. Lily-of-the-valley fragrance.

◄ *Stachyrus praecox* Leaves oval, pointed, mid-green. Growth open bush. Flowers small stiff bells carried in long clusters, drooping stems, before leaves appear. Pale yellow.

211

ORANGE & YELLOW
Small Flowers: Tall Plants

▲ *Adenocarpus decorticans* Leaves with three dark green, needle-like leaflets, clustered along stems. Flowers golden yellow, sweet-pea-like and clustered in terminal heads. Upper 'fan' petal kidney-shaped behind pouch or keel.

◄ *Acacia* hybrid 'Claire de Lune' (Mimosa, Wattle) Leaves long, narrow and spikey. Growth bushy, arching. Flowers in plumes of fluffy balls, encrusting one year old stems. Primrose yellow, somewhat fragrant.

◄ *Azara dentata* Leaves evergreen, deep green, glossy above, downy beneath, oval, toothed. Growth loose and shrubby. Flowers maize yellow. Thread-like petals clustered into fluffy knots, borne closely at ends of branches.

◄ *Buddleia globosa* (Orange Ball Tree) Leaves lance-shaped, pointed, corrugated, dark green above, buff beneath. Growth vigorous and erect. Flowers tubular, clustered into globular heads which are arranged in open spikes at the ends of the stems.

▲ *Caesalpina japonica* Leaves deeply divided into many small oval leaflets, fern-like, soft green. Stems armed with recurved spines. Growth lax, shrubby, usually seen against a wall. Flowers canary yellow, twenty to thirty together in open upright spikes.

◄ *Itea ilicifolia* Leaves oval, glossy evergreen, finely-toothed. Growth elegant, usually seen against a wall. Flowers pale creamy yellow borne in long hanging catkins. Fragrant.

▼ *Piptanthus laburnifolius* (Himalayan or Nepal Laburnum). Leaves trifoliate. Leaflets lance-shaped, pointed, hairy when young, glossy, dark green above. Growth lax. Flowers carried in terminal spikes among leaves. Sweet-pea-like, butter yellow.

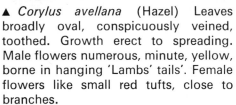

▲ *Corylus avellana* (Hazel) Leaves broadly oval, conspicuously veined, toothed. Growth erect to spreading. Male flowers numerous, minute, yellow, borne in hanging 'Lambs' tails'. Female flowers like small red tufts, close to branches.

▼ *Senecio grandifolius* Leaves large, oval, veined with jagged edges, borne horizontally Growth upright, little branched bushes. Flowers tiny yellow daisies borne in large rounded heads at ends of stems.

ORANGE & YELLOW
Medium Flowers: Small Plants

▲ *Schaueria calycotricha* Leaves smooth, broadly oval, on long stalks. Growth bushy, upstanding. Flowers primrose yellow two-lipped tubes held by green bristly (but soft) cups (calyces), borne in oblong spikes at the end of the branches.

◄ *Senecio laxifolius* Leaves oval, silvery-grey/green above, white beneath, evergreen. Growth dense, rounded. Flowers yellow, daisy-like, single, carried in profuse clusters above foliage.

ORANGE & YELLOW
Medium Flowers: Medium Plants

▶ *Desfontania spinosa* Leaves polished, evergreen, conspicuously veined and indented, each point armed with a prickle. Growth dense. Flowers long narrow, scarlet funnels, yellow at the mouth and within, hanging singly from the leaf axils.

▼ *Cassia corymbosa* (Senna Shrub) Leaves formed of two to three pairs of oval pale green leaflets. Growth lax, somewhat tender. Flowers golden yellow, five-petalled, opening flat and borne in terminal spikes.

▲ *Hibiscus* hybrid 'Lee Orange' Leaves broad, shining, jagged. Growth, shrubby. Flowers slightly twisted funnels. Five petals, burnt orange, etched with darker veins. Petals recurved. Protruding style like bottle brush.

▲ *Fremontia californica* Leaves dull green, rounded, three- to seven-lobed. Growth bushy, upright, often seen against a wall. Flowers showy, chalice-shaped, golden yellow. Five rounded, pointed petals.

◄ *Hypericum X inodorum* 'Elstead' (Syn. *elatum*) Leaves oval, in pairs, surrounding stem. Growth erect. Flowers bold shining yellow with five-pointed cups, flattening with age. Numerous yellow stamens. Salmon red, egg-shaped fruits follow.

217

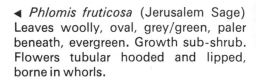
◄ *Phlomis fruticosa* (Jerusalem Sage) Leaves woolly, oval, grey/green, paler beneath, evergreen. Growth sub-shrub. Flowers tubular hooded and lipped, borne in whorls.

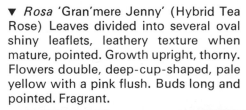
▼ *Rosa* 'Gran'mere Jenny' (Hybrid Tea Rose) Leaves divided into several oval shiny leaflets, leathery texture when mature, pointed. Growth upright, thorny. Flowers double, deep-cup-shaped, pale yellow with a pink flush. Buds long and pointed. Fragrant.

▼ *Rhododendron keysii* Leaves elliptical, bright green, evergreen, densely scaly, young ones curled back. Growth open. Clusters of long tubular bells with five-lipped recurved mouth. Cinnamon with yellow at tip and within.

▼ *Rhododendron wardii* Leaves round to oval, shiny, rich green, evergreen. Growth open. Flowers cup-shaped, primrose yellow. Buds tipped with pink. Five oval petals with crimson spot inside at base.

▲ *Rosa* 'Helen Traubel' (Hybrid Tea Rose). Leaves divided into oval, shining, pointed mid-green leaflets. Growth upright, thorny. Flowers double, pointed, deep-cut-shaped, packed with tightly overlapping petals, tips recurved. Deep apricot, suffused pink.

▲ *Rosa* 'Zambra' (Floribunda Rose) Leaves formed of oval, smooth, toothed, deep, glossy leaflets. Growth upright, prickly. Flowers semi-double, saucer-shaped. Petals recurved, burnt orange, yellow on the reverse.

◄ *Rosa* 'Ambrosia' (Single Floribunda Rose) Leaves formed of three or more oval, smooth, toothed leaflets. Growth upright, thorny. Flowers single. Several petals overlap. Copper orange, becoming mauve-tinted with age.

▲ *Rosa* 'Serenade' (Hybrid Tea Rose) Leaves with oval, smooth, polished coppery green leaflets. Growth upright, thorny. Flowers double, fragrant, deep-cup-shaped, packed with overlapping petals, tips of petals recurved.

SHRUBS
WHITE, GREEN & CREAM
Small Flowers: Small Plants

▼ *Cassiope* 'Muirhead' Leaves, tiny, carried close to the wiry stems, forming rope-like branches. Growth prostrate, mat forming. Flowers bell-like, pendulous, white, carried in profusion above foliage on very slender stems.

▼ *Daphne blagayana* (Daphne) Leaves oval, smooth, mid-green, evergreen. Growth, semi-prostrate. Flowers, rich cream, waxy, highly fragrant, borne in terminal clusters. Tubular, mouth flaring into four pointed lobes.

▲ *Cornus sanguinea* (Common Dogwood, Cornel) Leaves oval, pointed, smooth, wavy-edged, veins in pairs, turning red in autumn. Flowers with four narrow pointed petals, borne in clusters.

▼ *Daphne laureola* (Spurge Laurel) Leaves oval, shiny, dark green, leathery, evergreen. A low growing bush. Flowers tubular, fragrant, with four rounded lobes, yellow/green.

◀ *Epigaea repens* Leaves, evergreen, oval, leathery, dark green. Growth creeping and mat-forming. Flowers pink or white, fragrant, borne in clusters, partially hidden among leaves, tubular with five, broad pointed petals.

▶ *Erica carnea* 'Alba' (White Heather) Leaves needle-like, dark green, shining, clothing stems closely. Growth mat forming. Flowers borne in one-sided spike, numerous narrow creamy-white bells. Brown stamens showing at mouth.

▲ *Ribes laurifolium* Leaves, oval to long oval, pointed, leathery, bright green, evergreen, slightly toothed. Growth open, shrubby. Flowers tubular, male hanging clusters, female in smaller, erect clusters. Greenish-yellow with five petal-like lobes.

▲ *Gaulnettya X wisleyensis* 'Wisley Pearl'. Leaves oval, dark green, pointed, evergreen. Growth compact. Flowers numerous, globular, hanging bells, pure white with cream calyces.

▶ *Helianthemum* 'The Bride' (Rock Rose). Leaves, long, narrow, grey green, central vein. Growth prostrate, mat forming. Flowers floppy and frail, saucer-shaped, borne very freely. Five rounded cream/white petals, yellow patch at base.

WHITE, GREEN & CREAM
Small Flowers: Medium Plants

▶ *Choisya ternata* (Mexican Orange Blossom). Leaves bright green, exceptionally glossy, oval, carried in threes. Growth rounded. Flowers five separate oval petals. Central cluster of yellow stamens, fragrant, borne in loose clusters.

▼ *Abeliophyllum distichum* Leaves oval, pointed, appearing after flowers. Growth open. Flowers clustered along bare branches, white, tubular with orange centres. Five strap-shaped petals.

▼ *Cistus X cyprius* (Rock Rose) Leaves sticky, narrowly oval, pointed. Growth shrubby. Flowers saucer-shaped, eventually flat. Five broad petals, pure white with basal maroon blotch. Boss of golden stamens.

▲ *Melicope ternata* (Wharangi) Leaves trifoliate, oval, thick, shining. Growth graceful. Flowers almost insignificant, cream, borne close to branches, four-petalled with prominent central style.

▲ *Fabiana imbricata* Leaves scale-like, overlapping, evergreen, medium to yellow green. Growth plume-like. Flowers waxy, white. Long slender trumpets often borne in great abundance.

◄ *Leycesteria formosa* (Himalayan Honeysuckle) Leaves oval to heart-shaped, shiny. Growth erect, with hollow stems. Flowers cream, tubular, borne among conspicuous pink triangular bracts in hanging chains.

▲ *Fothergilla major* Leaves oval, fluted with veins, glossy-green, red, orange, yellow at end of season. Growth compact. Flowers borne in spikes, like creamy bottle brushes, fragrant, plentiful.

▼ *Nandina domestica* (Chinese Bamboo, Heavenly Bamboo) Leaves divided into several or many elliptic, pointed leaflets, red flushed when young. Growth open, graceful. Flowers upstanding.

▲ *Olearia gunniana* (Otway Daisy Bush) Leaves narrow, oblong, slightly toothed, grey/green. Growth, compact, rounded. Flowers, daisy-like, white with brownish-yellow central disc, borne in branching clusters. Many flowers together.

▶ *Pimelea spectabilis* Leaves small, narrow, slender, pointed, clothing length of branches. Growth bushy. Flowers carried in distinctive globular heads, white, tubular with flaring mouth.

▼ *Myrtus luma* (Syn. *M. apiculata* and *Eugenia apiculata*) Leaves oval, pointed, small. Growth dense. Bark flakes when mature, revealing cinnamon patches. Flowers white, small, profuse, bowl-shaped, filled with slender white stamens.

▼ *Philadelphus* 'Avalanche' (Mock Orange, erroneously Syringa) Leaves oval, pointed, prominently veined, somewhat toothed. Growth on mature bushes arching and semi-pendent. Flowers fragrant, borne in clusters, bowl-shaped, golden stamens at centre.

▼ *Stephanandra tanakae* Leaves, broadly oval, prominently sharply toothed, deeply fluted by veins. Growth graceful, with arching stems. Flowers tiny, green/cream, borne in loose terminal sprays. Five petals.

▲ *Philadelphus* 'Virginal' (Mock Orange, erroneously Syringa) Leaves oval, pointed, prominently veined, somewhat toothed. Growth arching on mature bushes. Flowers double, bowl-shaped, filled with overlapping petals.

▼ *Sarcococca confusa* Leaves thick, shining, oval, pointed, evergreen with marked central rib. Growth dense. Flowers fragrant, three or four together in leaf axils, back petals, being composed of four white fleshy stamens only.

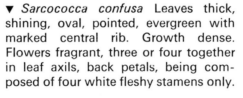

▲ *Osmarea X burkwoodii* Leaves evergreen, leathery, elliptic. Growth dense, with arching stems. Flowers very fragrant, borne in leaf axils, towards ends of lateral stems. Small, white, like four-petalled stars.

227

▲ *Viburnum tomentosum* 'Lanarth Variety' Leaves oval, sharply toothed. Growth bushy, with horizontal branches. Flowers borne along upper surface of branches like snow. White broad-petalled sterile flowers frill edge of flower-head. Smaller, fertile flowers in middle.

▼ *Skimmia japonica* Leaves oval, glossy, with marked central rib, evergreen, aromatic when crushed. Growth open, erect and bushy. Flowers, male and female on separate bushes. Berries red.

▲ *Spiraea thunbergii* Leaves dainty, long, narrow. Growth arching, open, bushy. Flowers pure white, starry, very small, borne in profusion along branches. Five petals.

▼ *Viburnum X burkwoodii* (Viburnum) Leaves oval, edges slightly toothed. Growth rounded, much-branched. Flowers fragrant, white, waxy, borne in rounded clusters. Buds pink. Five petals.

◄ *Viburnum opulus sterile* (Snowball Tree, Guelder Rose) Leaves three lobed, edges notched, paler beneath, good autumn colour. Growth rounded, spreading. Flowers tightly packed into white balls. Five petals.

WHITE, GREEN & CREAM
Small Flowers: Tall Plants

▲ *Garrya elliptica* (Silk Tassel Bush) Leaves dark green, oval, shining, edges crimped, evergreen. Growth dense, often as a wall shrub. Flowers grey/green, borne in long, hanging tassels.,

▼ *Hydrangea sargentiana* Leaves velvety, downy, oval, large. Growth bushy, with bristly stems. Flowers borne in flat heads, outer ones four-petalled, white forming a frill around small tight bluish flowers in centre.

▶ *Holodiscus discolor* (Syn. *Spiraea discolor*) Leaves hoary green, lightly felted beneath, oval, pointed. Growth open, elegant, with arching stems. Flowers cream, minute, forming conspicuous graceful plumes at stem tips.

◄ *Hydrangea paniculata* Leaves oval, pointed, heart-shaped at base, smooth, entire. Growth upright, arching. Flowers carried on stem tips in cone-like heads. Chalk white four petalled sterile flowers held above small cream fluffy ones.

▼ *Muehlenbeckia complexa* (Wire Vine) Leaves kidney-shaped or oval. Growth tangled, wiry dark stems. Flowers insignificant, followed by lobed cup-shaped white fruits, with black club-like seed in the centre.

◄ *Ligustrum ovalifolium* (Privet) Leaves shining, oval, pointed, marked central vein, tendency to 'fold'. Growth upright. Flowers tubular, small, heavily fragrant, somewhat sickly, four-petalled, cream, many carried in terminal, pyramidal heads.

▲ *Olearia macrodonta* (Daisy Bush) Leaves large, grey/green, resembling blunt, spined holly leaves, evergreen. Growth compact. Flowers chalk white, daisy-like, borne in dense clusters, often obscuring leaves.

▲ *Pittosporum tobira* Leaves oval, leathery, shining dark green. Growth rounded, twiggy. Flowers waxy, cream, tubular. Fragrance like orange blossom. Five strap-shaped petals.

◄ *Neopanax colensoi* (Mountain Five Finger). Leaves large hand-shaped, with three to five oval, glossy, dark green leaflets. Growth erect to somewhat spreading, bushy. Flowers green, tiny, borne in loose, large clusters among upper leaves.

▼ *Sambucus nigra aurea* (Golden Elder, Elderberry) Leaves divided into several elliptical, green leaflets. Growth rounded. Flowers sickly fragrant, small, borne in large flat or convex heads. Five petals, fused into short tube at base.

▲ *Poncirus trifoliata* (Japanese Bitter Orange) Leaves sparse, three narrow, oval leaflets together. Growth, tangled, stems green, spiny, somewhat angled and flattened. Flowers fragrant. Five petals somewhat ragged, on bare stems.

▲ *Staphylea colchica* (Bladder Nut) Leaves divided into three or five smooth, elliptical, pointed leaflets with finely-toothed margins. Growth vigorous. Flowers cream, like miniature daffodils.

▲ *Syringa* 'Mme. Lemoine' (White Lilac) Leaves heart-shaped, pointed, smooth. Growth open and erect. Flowers borne in bold terminal sprays, often several together. White, fragrant, double.

▲ *Sobaria aitchisonii* Leaves divided into several elliptic, pointed, leaflets like those of ash tree. Grows shrubby. Flowers small, many together in fluffy white plume. Five rounded petals. Stamens fluffy.

◄ *Spiraea nipponica rotundifolia* Leaves broadly oval to round, smooth, rather sparse. Growth twiggy and arching. Flowers clustered into dense conical heads, mostly towards the ends of arching branches. Five rounded petals. Fluffy stamens.

WHITE, GREEN & CREAM
Medium Flowers: Small Plants

◄ *Hebe macrantha* (Shrubby Veronica) Leaves thick, oval, with small rounded teeth arranged in opposite pairs close to stem. Growth rather sparse. Flowers pure white, showy, composed of four oval petals fused at base.

▲ *Halimiocistus X sahucii* Leaves evergreen, small, narrow and lance-shaped. Growth slender and lax. Flowers shallow bowl-shaped. Five distinct petals, each rounded to triangular. Boss of golden stamens.

WHITE, GREEN & CREAM
Medium Flowers: Medium Plants

► *Rhododendron* 'Silver Slipper' (Knaphill Azalea) Leaves oval, copper-flushed when young, dark green later. Growth compact and rounded. Flowers white flushed with pink, decorative, showy, several in a head. Five rounded petals, upper one feathered orange. Upsweeping long prominent stamens.

▲ *Carpenteria californica* Leaves elliptic, rich glossy green, evergreen. Growth erect to spreading, bushy. Flowers saucer-shaped. Five pure white broad petals surrounding pom-pom of golden stamens.

▲ *Gordonia lasianthus* Leaves large, oval, dark green, paler beneath. Growth rounded and compact. Flowers cup-shaped with five petals, often rolled at edge, holding splendid boss of deep golden stamens. Fragrant.

◄ *Exochorda giraldii* Leaves oval, pointed, pinkish tinged when young. Growth erect to spreading. Flowers with five rounded petals white. Yellow stamens at centre. Borne in loose profusion along branches.

235

▲ *Stewartia ovata* (Syn. *Stuartia ovata*)
Leaves long, oval pointed, downy
beneath. Growth compact. Flowers like
shallow cream-white saucer, with conspicuous boss of golden stamens.

▶ *Rosa spinosissima* (Burnet Rose)
Leaves divided into three or five pairs of
leaflets, oval, toothed with very prickly
stems. Growth bristly. Flowers single.
Five broad creamy white petals. Golden
stamens.

▼ *Rosa rugosa albo-plena* 'Blanc
Double de Coubert' Leaves oval, puckered, toothed dark shining green. Growth
dense and prickly. Flowers white, semi
double, opening flat. Petals variable.
(Red and pink forms of *Rosa rugosa* are
frequent.)

▲ *Rosa* 'Iceberg' (Floribunda Rose)
Leaves divided into five to seven oval,
glossy, toothed leaflets. Growth vigorous and thorny. Flowers in clusters. Pure
white petals opening wide, cup-shaped,
fragrant. Buds long, slender and pointed.

◄ *Rubus* 'Tridel' Leaves triangular in outline, three-lobed with toothed edge, mid-green, paler beneath. Growth arching, thornless. Flowers glistening white. Five broad saucer-shaped petals with neatly scalloped edges. Central boss of golden stamens.

WHITE, GREEN & CREAM
Medium Flowers: Tall Plants

▶ *Styrax hemsleyana* Leaves oval, shining green with toothed edges. Growth graceful. Flowers pendent, white, thick-textured. Five long petals in shallow bell formation with central sheaf of stamens.

◄ *Camellia japonica* 'Tricolor' (Camellia) Leaves glossy, oval, thick, evergreen, toothed. Growth dense and rounded. Flowers semi-double. Broad white overlapping petals sometimes flecked with pink and red. Sheaf of golden stamens.

▼ *Styrax japonica* Leaves oval, shining green. Growth graceful and arching. Flowers white and waxy, pendent. Five long petals in star formation.

WHITE, GREEN & CREAM
Large Flowers: Medium Plants

► *Paeonia suffruticosa* 'Rock's Variety' (Tree peony) Leaves greyish/green, divided into several oval points. Growth erect to spreading with robust branched stems. Flowers semi-double, white, with dramatic seven-pointed central star in maroon/purple. Silky golden boss of stamens.

SHRUBS
BLUE
Small Flowers:
Small Plants

▲ *Caryopteris X clandonensis* (Blue Spiraea) Leaves soft, narrow, grey/green with serrated edges. Flowers small, borne in dense clusters from the upper leaf axils, deep lavender blue, tubular with narrow petals and pin-like stamens.

◄ *Vinca major* (Periwinkle, Sorcerer's Violet) Leaves evergreen, oval, pointed, smooth. Growth arching and trailing, often rooting. Flowers with five square-topped petals, slightly twisted and creating a propellor shape. Clear violet blue.

BLUE
Small Flowers: Small Plants

▲ *Perovskia atriplicifolia* (Russian Sage) Leaves with sage-like aroma, grey/green, narrowly oval, coarsely-toothed, in opposite pairs on erect stems. Stems and leaves silvery white, downy. Flowers tubular, small, blue/violet, borne in slender, branched spikes.

▶ *Rosmarinus officinalis* (Rosemary) Leaves long, narrow, almost needle-like, dark bright green above, pale beneath, aromatic, evergreen and carried the length of the stem. Flowers grey/blue, borne amid leaves on upper part of stem, tubular, lipped mouth.

◀ *Ceanothus arboreus* 'Trewithen Blue' (Californian Tree Lilac) Leaves oval, glossy, prominently veined. Flowers borne in compact rounded clusters, in profusion, each flower minute. Five clear blue petals, with dark eye.

BLUE
Small Flowers: Tall Plants

◄ *Syringa vulgaris* 'Firmament' (Lilac) Leaves heart-shaped, pointed, smooth, pale green. Flowers small, tubular carrried in profusion in slightly elongated rounded clusters, very fragrant. Four-petalled, sky blue.

▲ *Ceanothus thyrsiflorus* Leaves dark green, somewhat shining, oval, plentiful, evergreen. Usually grown as a wall shrub. Flowers clear blue, minute, five-petalled, in dense club-shaped clusters towards the tips of the shoots.

BLUE
Medium Flowers: Medium Plants

► *Hydrangea macrophylla* 'Hortensia' (Common Hydrangea) Leaves oval, pointed, bright green, strongly veined and toothed. Flowers carried in large mop-heads atop stems. Four (sometimes five) petals, broad and bluntly-pointed. Often pink, mauve or blue.

SHRUBS
PURPLE & LILAC
Small Flowers: Small Plants

▶ *Hebe* 'Autumn Glory' (Shrubby veronica) Leaves evergreen, oval, shiny, carried thickly in pairs on alternate sides of the stem. Flowers purple in spike-like heads. Unopened buds at the top silvery.

▲ *Daphne Mezereum* (Garland Flower Mezereon) Flowers before leaves, thickly covering branches. Leaves lance-shaped, light green, hairless. Flowers highly fragrant, rose purple. Four petals, opening wide from narrow tube.

▼ *Erica tetralix* (Cross-leaved Heather) Leaves narrow, small, spikey, grey/green and carried in whorls of four. Flowers mauve-pink in clusters at the top of the upright branches, papery, bell-like, nodding. Tiny brown stamens.

▼ *Lavandula spica* (Old English Lavender) Leaves evergreen, grey, long, narrow and highly aromatic. Flowers blue/mauve, borne in long spike-like terminal heads on square upstanding stems.

PURPLE & LILAC
Small Flowers: Medium Plants

▶ *Hebe* 'Midsummer Beauty' (Shrubby Veronica) Leaves evergreen, shining, narrowly oval and pointed. Flowers borne in long bottle brush-like spikes. Four purple, tubular petals opening wide with long protruding stamens.

PURPLE & LILAC
Small Flowers: Tall Plants

◄ *Buddleia davidii* (Butterfly Bush) Leaves long, narrow, pointed, strongly veined, mid-green, paler beneath. Flowers purple, densely clustered into long tapering spikes, very attractive to butterflies. Heavy scent.

▲ *Syringa vulgaris* 'Sensation' (Lilac) Leaves broadly oval, pointed, very smooth, pale green. Flowers carried in large clustered heads, usually three or four borne together at end of stem, very fragrant. Four-petalled.

PURPLE & LILAC
Medium Flowers: Medium Plants

▶ *Feijoa sellowiana* Leaves leathery, oval, dark and shining above, grey/green beneath. Flowers crimson and white. Petals fleshy and edible, like cowrie shells, darker within and clustered round a sheaf of pin-like brown/purple stamens with pinkish brown heads.

▼ *Hibiscus syriacus* 'Coelestis' Leaves deeply lobed, oval, shining, mid-green. Flowers showy, opening flat. Five light mauve-blue petals marked crimson at base. Central stamen column cream, club-like.

▼ *Hibiscus syriacus* 'Blue Bird' Leaves deeply-lobed, oval, somewhat shining, mid-green. Flowers showy, like blue saucers, blotched purple at base of each of the five petals. Buds purple. Central stalked club of stamens.

▶ *Hydrangea serrata* 'Lilacina' (Lace-cap Hydrangea) Leaves long, oval, pointed, finely-toothed. Flowers carried in flat terminal heads, the outer flowers pale lilac. Four large petals surround the small starry mauve flowers in the centre.

PURPLE & LILAC
Medium Flowers:
Tall Plants

▲ *Hydrangea villosa* Leaves lance-shaped, pointed, edge undulating or slightly toothed, velvety and downy. Flowers mauve-blue, becoming pink with age. Outer florets large and four-petalled with flat heads of tiny mauve flowers in centre.

▲ *Rhododendron* 'Susan' Leaves ever-green, long, oval, blunt-tipped, dark green and shining marked central vein. Flowers bluish-mauve in showy rounded heads of radiating trumpet-like flowers. Petals flared and frilled at mouth.

Botanical Name Index

Common Name Index